30 DAYS TO A NEW YOU

STEPS TO UNSHAKABLE FAITH AND FREEDOM

STEVE CIOCCOLANTI

Dedicated to my children
Alexis, Austin, Amberay and Alaska

and to all who long for a
father, mentor and model.

30 Days to a New You: Steps to Unshakable Faith and Freedom

Published by Discover Media www.discover.org.au

Cover design by Selena Sok selena@discover.org.au

© 2012-2021 Steve Cioccolanti www.discoverchurch.online

Unless otherwise noted, all Scripture quotations are taken from New King James Version of the Bible. Copyright © 1979, 1980, 1982. Used by permission of Thomas Nelson, Inc., Publishers.

Scripture quotations marked:

Goodspeed are from Edgar J. Goodspeed's The New Testament: An American Translation.

GWT are from the God's Word Translation version of the Bible.

ISV from International Standard Version.

Knox are from The New Testament in the Translation of Ronald Knox.

Moffatt are from the James Moffatt's The New Testament: A New Translation.

NAS are taken from the New American Standard Bible. © 1995. Used by permission of The Lockman Foundation.

NEB are from the New English Bible.

NET are from the New English Translation.

NIV are from the New International Version. © 1973, 1978, 1984. Used by permission of International Bible Society.

NLT are from the New Living Translation © 1996.

Used by permission of Tyndale House Publishers.

Phillips are from J.B. Phillips' The New Testament in Modern English.

Taylor are from Kenneth Taylor's paraphrases of the New Testament.

Paperback ISBN 978-0-9873617-6-9

Ebook ISBN 978-0-9873617-9-0

Printed in U.S.A.

1

INTRODUCING THE 30 DAY PLAN

Day 1

*Y*our Freedom is Within Reach
When God wants to revolutionize your life, He starts by changing the way you see yourself and the way you speak about yourself. This book lays out the steps I took to become free from various self-limiting beliefs and self-defeating behaviors and, more importantly, to maintain my freedom. Without this transformation, I could not have become the person God wanted me to be today. I have the privilege to minister to thousands of people at a time even though I used to have a fear of public speaking; I lead an amazing team which produces documentaries and videos even though my degree is unrelated to film making; and I have not only survived but thrived during challenges which would have crushed and demoralized the old me before I became a Christian.

I can tell you the message of this book worked for me long before I experienced any of the victories I am describing to you. The instructions work because they are all based on God's instructions to us in the Bible. Faith is following instructions before you obtain results.

Imagine your hope for a beautiful life is standing on one side of a great chasm, and the reality of your destiny is waiting for you on the other side, what is it that connects your hope to your destiny? It's a three-fold cable that everybody possesses. Everybody, no matter how rich or poor, has equal access to these connectors. The three-fold cable is comprised of your thoughts, words and actions.

Motivational speakers and life coaches talk about the power of positive thinking and positive speaking, but very few of their fans can duplicate their success. Why? One reason is it's based on will power, rather than God's power. The person who is feeling like a failure doesn't need to be told they need to change. They already know that! They need the *power* to change. They also need more than inspiration, they need clear instructions. What exactly are the thoughts we should think and words we should speak? God's instructions are a level above the very best a life coach has to offer.

There is also a lot of talk about goal-setting, and I believe it's valuable. I have written down goals every year. But I have achieved far more than I could have imagined without paying much attention to my own goals. Don't pay attention to goals - pay attention to God! God will change *who* you are before He changes *what* you have. By paying close attention to God, I had for the first time in my life a Perfect Role Model. I started to change my own thoughts and words. I craved to think and speak in line with God's ways. Rather than starting with the goals you want, start with the person that you are right now. Before I ever saw myself as a leader, entrepreneur or author, I needed to see myself the way God sees me. This is the crucial step many people miss on their way to trying to reach their goals. This crucial step is what I want you to undertake for the next 30 days.

*R*esults You Can Expect

As a Christian mentor, I've coached people to see themselves from God's perspective and the results are duplicatable. I am humbled to receive testimonies like these:

> *My relationship with colleagues broke down because of my lack of confidence and fear of failure deep inside. I worried a lot about people's attitude and thoughts about me, but...I now speak with my colleagues with confidence and forgave those words they used to hurt me as they didn't know what they were doing without God in their life. I not only perform well on my job but I have also started to enjoy myself at workplace. God's love is so real and abundant toward me. — Shelley, Australia*

> *As a new Christian, I was previously afraid that God no longer cared about me, but I was no longer afraid after following the 30 day plan in your book! It gave me the stability I needed as a Christian that I was missing before. I've read many Christian books on faith and miracles, but when I practiced exactly what you wrote and meditated on the specific scriptures you used, it was the first time I felt something in me rose up, it was like I could face and defeat anything that comes my way. It felt like a*

complete breakthrough and gave me a different level of faith that didn't fade at all. — Josephine, Singapore

66 *All you said about your father, smoking and poor self-image are the things that are happening in my life. I've been following your plan for 2 months. Now my dad and I are close to each other. I don't have to worry about anything anymore because I have Jesus in my life. Last week my devout Catholic aunty really surprised me when she said she was proud of me and that she loves the 'new me' and admires my faith. She even told me that she had a lot of things to learn from me. Ohh, how the Lord is strong. I never thought or dreamed that one day my devout aunty would tell me that she had to learn from me. — Michelle, Mauritius*

66 *From now on, I know that I don't have to fear anything because Jesus lives in me and He didn't give me a spirit of fear. — Paul, Malaysia*

🦋 🦋 🦋

The 30 Day Plan

Their successes were not easy, but you can see it's entirely possible if you make the decision right now to stick to the plan. You will not just copy what I did. You will understand *why* I did it and *why* you may want to follow it, too. Each day you should read only one chapter and ponder on it. Chapter 1 which you are reading represents your first step on Day 1.

Find something in each chapter that excites you and let

it refresh and renew your thinking. When you get to chapter 5, you should be at Day 5.

Chapters 5 through 9 contain the Scripture Prayers that form the main components of your Meditation Plan. If you spend only 24 days meditating on these five chapters, you will arrive at Day 28. Once you've followed that plan, and only after you follow that plan, I recommend your reading the last two chapters. They will take you to Day 29 and Day 30 respectively.

The message of this book has helped many people build their sense of identity, self-worth, and self-confidence, but it is not a self-help book. Just as you cannot teach yourself (you already know what you know), so too you cannot really help yourself. True help does not come from self, but from the Helper – the Holy Spirit. Jesus said, "But the Helper, the Holy Spirit, whom the Father will send in My name, He will teach you all things, and bring to your remembrance all things that I said to you" (John 14:26). Self-help is only natural and temporary; the Holy Spirit's help is supernatural and eternal.

❧ ❧ ❧

My Personal Story

Obviously many people, even after they become Christian, struggle with inner conflicts, purity of lifestyle and purpose in life. How do we cooperate with the transforming power of the Holy Spirit? That's what this little book is about. If I of all people can overcome, then you can overcome. If I can succeed, be assured you can succeed.

You see, before I was born, my father had already decided he did not want to be responsible for his wife or his daughter (my older sister). When he came back for a brief period, I was the accident. Before I was born, I had already been wounded with a spirit of rejection. It was not the best introduction to life that a baby could have.

As I grew up, my father was absent and never supported my Down Syndrome sister's health nor my education. I would get a letter once a year for my birthday, and the most he ever gave was $20. My mother worked hard to support us as a single mum. I grew up mad at the whole world. Even though I excelled in school through my mother's loving encouragement, I walked about with a victim mentality. How could a young man like me ever succeed in life?

Little did I know that I was on the devil's fast track to destruction. As soon as I got a taste of freedom at the age of 18, my behavior quickly spun out of control. I tried every drug imaginable except those that required needles (I don't like needles). I smoked everything that I could light. I also changed many girlfriends to fill the gaps in my broken soul. In my effort to be less like my father, I was becoming more like him. How could I escape this trap?

The cocktail of sins I was living in finally made me numb emotionally and spiritually. I was falling into depression and had no rope to hold on to. I tried every kind of music to soothe myself – from reggae to Mongolian chants, from the Beastie Boys to Led Zeppelin. I read up on the occult and quantum physics. I enrolled in university classes on Buddhism and Chinese philosophy, even though I didn't think they could lead me to a job which would make any money. I was looking for answers. How do people stay sane in an insane world?

Never did I think to look at the Bible for answers. In fact, the Bible may be the worst book in the world for someone to read if he has not first humbly asked God to open his eyes. The Pharisees were a case in point. They read from a dry, lifeless, intellectual point of view. But the Bible is alive and powerful, sharper than any two-edged sword (Hebrews 4:12). The Bible is a two-edged sword because it has a way of blessing its friends and confusing its enemies.

Reading the Bible when I was a critical faultfinder would have only confused me. But while I was on one of my trips to Thailand, some people introduced me to the Gospel of Christ in a rational and powerful way. It convinced me that I was the very kind of person Jesus came to rescue. A new glow came into my heart after I genuinely felt sorry for my sins and trusted in Jesus to not condemn me on the Day of Judgment. I suddenly wanted to read the Bible for myself. For some reason, it was the first time I decided to take my elementary school Bible (given to all students by Episcopalian nuns) with me on this particular trip.

After I realized I was a man lost at sea, I came to appreciate the Bible as my life-saver and North Star. When you see yourself as a man parched in blazing heat, the Bible becomes a fountain of fresh, living water. When you see yourself as a man starved to the point of death, every verse in the Bible becomes a delicacy that you relish.

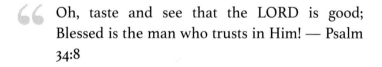

> Oh, taste and see that the LORD is good; Blessed is the man who trusts in Him! — Psalm 34:8

When I first got saved in Thailand, I quickly led another half-Thai, half-*farang* (*Caucasian* in Thai) to the Lord. We were Bible-reading buddies. A missionary once saw us so consumed with reading the Bible, she advised us, "You're just in the honeymoon stage. We all start out reading the Bible like you. But soon the honeymoon stage will be over." Thank God, the honeymoon still isn't over for me after two decades! My appetite for the Bible has grown over the years. I understand the Bible better now. I see more truths now. And the more truths I see, the freer I can be!

When I meet people who don't subscribe to any religion, oftentimes they say to me, "I'm not interested in your Christianity. I'm a free thinker." I ask them, "Do you think I'm bound? Do I look like I'm in bondage? I'm also a freethinker. I'm free to think too. But did you know you can be *more* free?" Every time I've asked that question, they always look like a new thought has just entered their head. "Really?" they ask with curiosity. "Of course," I tell them, "you can be more free. Jesus said, 'You shall know the truth and the truth shall make you free' (John 8:32). Freedom is based on the amount of truth you know and apply. That means the more truth you know, the freer you will be."

If the ultimate freedom comes through knowing the truth, then the logical question is, "Which truths exactly should we start at?" The Bible may seem like a big book to a beginner. Where do you start if you need to overcome specific habits, bondages or sins? Many Christians turn to famous preachers, best-selling authors, or extra-Biblical commentaries to make sense of the Bible. Sometimes they are safe and helpful; other times they confuse the reader even more. Too many Christians still have not obtained the lasting freedom they are looking for.

When I became Christian, I fed myself with only good Christian books. My definition of a good Christian book is this: 1) it drives me to hunger for the Word of God while I'm reading it, 2) the Holy Spirit gives me a sense of spiritual peace while I'm reading it. From my earliest Christian walk, I devoured truth. Church leaders recommended books to me and I read most of them. I also bought a lot of Christian books and read most of them. I read everything that exalted

God's Word and that I felt the Holy Spirit permitted me to study.

Once in a while, my spirit didn't feel right about a book, so I would just let it sit on my shelf. Only years later did I find out that some of those books I skipped contained theological, scientific or factual errors. After I matured in my head, I discovered what my heart knew all along – some books aren't worth my time because they are men's opinions and deny the Word of God. Thank God for the Holy Spirit's leading even when we're young Christians!

One of the good Christian books I read taught that there are more than 100 Scriptures in the New Testament which describes what God thinks of me. They usually contain the words "in Christ," "in Him," "by Him," "through Him," and such phrases. These Scriptures explain who I am, what I have, and what I can do because of what Jesus has done for me. This was an invaluable revelation. It was like discovering a mine of concentrated truths which I needed right away.

What I did next changed my life: I personally looked up nearly 70 of those 100 Scriptures. They were enough for me to change in a radical way. They were just what I needed to build myself up spiritually. I wrote them down. I made personal prayers out of them. I spoke them out loud every day for more than 30 days. I believe you can break an old habit and form a new one if you consistently do something new for 30 days! I did it for 30 days and beyond.

My personality changed. I stopped being easily upset and started enjoying life. I stopped thinking about myself first and started caring more about other people. Helping people became a pleasure. Traveling just to visit places no longer appealed to me as much as travelling to meet people and bring Christ's healing to their lives.

My habits changed. I stopped smoking, not because

some religious rule forced me to stop, but because I felt *clean on the inside*. I didn't care to look at porn any more. Human nakedness became sacred. I understood sex was designed by God as a gift reserved for marriage. I saw porn as demeaning to God's precious daughters. What was happening to me? What was once an addiction became disgusting. My taste buds even changed! I started eating healthier food before medical research decided what was healthy. I started preferring kosher ingredients before I knew what the Jewish term *kosher* meant. (No, I don't believe we have to eat a kosher diet to go to Heaven. "For the kingdom of God is not eating and drinking, but righteousness and peace and joy in the Holy Spirit." Romans 14:17) I was healthier, happier and spiritually stronger. My prayer life flourished - I prayed and got answers. Yes, God actually wants to hear and answer my prayers! My relationship with God became more than getting a sermon once a week, it stayed with me day to day, week to week. A relationship is two-way. I not only trust Christ, but I also know Christ trusts me.

*W*ell Done on Day 1!

By the very fact that you have picked up this book, I believe this is the kind of change you are looking for – a life change! I would never attribute my previously scarred personality and twisted outlook on life to my father's irresponsibility to our family alone, but the more I meet others who are struggling, the more aware I have become of how deep childhood wounds affect adults. There is no lasting help in self-help; you and I really need the Holy Spirit's help.

You have taken a wonderful first step! Well done on finishing Day 1 to a new you! Take this day to reflect on what you have just learned, what struck a chord inside you, what excited you the most. Then make a decision to apply what you learn in this little book for the next 30 days. It may help you to pray this prayer of commitment to God:

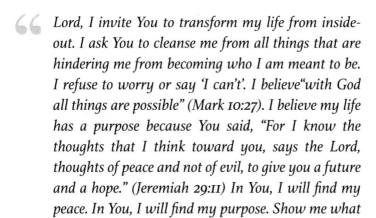

> *Lord, I invite You to transform my life from inside-out. I ask You to cleanse me from all things that are hindering me from becoming who I am meant to be. I refuse to worry or say 'I can't'. I believe"with God all things are possible" (Mark 10:27). I believe my life has a purpose because You said, "For I know the thoughts that I think toward you, says the Lord, thoughts of peace and not of evil, to give you a future and a hope." (Jeremiah 29:11) In You, I will find my peace. In You, I will find my purpose. Show me what You think about me and how I can be more like You. Thank You.*

You can get what I got if you do what I did. After two decades of practicing and sharing these truths, I can say this book contains the most compact and most user-friendly steps I know to build a strong personality, break addictive habits, and grow up spiritually in the shortest time possible. I speak not from theory alone, but from personal experience. I humbly offer this program to you and pray its blessings will remain with you until you become all God created you to be!

2

WHAT'S THE BIG MYSTERY?

Day 2

*G*od's Mystery ~ Once Concealed, Now Revealed!
If asked to explain why Jesus came to earth, many Christians would struggle to answer with Scriptures or would merely point out that the Good News is: "Jesus came to forgive sins." Thank God for the forgiveness of sins, sinners need to be forgiven, but did you know the forgiveness of sins was already available under the old covenant?

Sure! That was how the Old Testament saints got saved. They believed in the *coming* Messiah who was predicted in prophecy and illustrated by the blood sacrifices of old. We believe in Messiah who *came* fulfilling the prophecies and gave the ultimate blood sacrifice of all. We all get saved the same way: they looked forward to the Promise; we look backward to the Fulfillment.

But there is a difference between the Old Testament and the New Testament. What is it? The difference is not in God; He never changes (Malachi 3:6). The difference is not in the devil; he also doesn't seem to change, at least in the sense of improving. Jesus said, "He was a murderer from the beginning, and does not stand in the truth, because there is no truth in him. When he speaks a lie, he speaks from his own resources, for he is a liar and the father of it" (John 8:44). In other words, he's the same old devil.

What is it that makes the New Covenant "new" and "better" (Hebrew 8:6)? Clearly there is a big difference between Old Testament believers and New Testament believers. The greatest mystery that has been hidden for ages from all of God's holy angels and from all the Old Testament prophets, but is *now revealed* to us New Testament believers, was first introduced by the Incarnation.

The Incarnation introduced the mystery that God could actually live in human flesh! No other major religion in the world dares to claim that God can live inside us. How is that possible? Jesus was the first Person to demonstrate the possibility of this mysterious union. He was and remains forever fully God and fully man. He continues to live in Heaven with a fully physical body like our own, but glorified and indestructible. (That fact alone tells us how physically real Heaven is, it is a physical world just like ours, only perfect.) While Jesus stands in a class of His own, He did not think we are worthless and pitiful. Far from it! He sent the same Holy Spirit who lived inside of Him to come live inside of us! His death, burial and resurrection paved the way for any believer to receive His divine nature as well.

 By which [knowledge of Christ] have been given
to us exceedingly great and precious promises,

that through these you may be PARTAKERS of
the DIVINE NATURE..." — 2 Peter 1:4

No, we are certainly not God, but God does live in us who
are born again believers. Eternal life is ours. God the Father
wanted us to be conformed to the image of His dear Son,
that Jesus might be the *first*born among many brethren
(Romans 8:29). If Jesus was the *first*, then there also must be a
second, a third, and many more. Jesus was to be the first
among many "brothers just like Him."

This mystery is a terrifying weapon against the devil and
his "weakness message." Christians need to know that when
they became Christian, they did not merely become forgiven
sinners, but they became "new creations in Christ" (2
Corinthians 5:17); they became the temple for Almighty God
to dwell in (1 Corinthians 3:16). Paul preached this original
Gospel:

The MYSTERY which has been hidden from ages and
from generations, but now has been revealed to His saints.
To them God willed to make known what are the riches of
the glory of this MYSTERY among the Gentiles: which is
CHRIST IN YOU, the hope of glory. — Colossians 1:26-27

Even the Apostle Peter recognized that what Paul
preached was "hard to be understood," yet completely
necessary lest we twist the Scriptures (dumb it down,
dilute its power) and fall "to our own destruction" (2 Peter
3:16). Hosea 4:6 is often quoted, "My people are destroyed
for lack of knowledge." I like to combine Hosea 4:6 with 2
Peter 3:16 and say, "My people are destroyed for lack of
knowledge, especially when they lack knowledge of what
Paul taught in the New Testament." Peter said we risk
being destroyed when we don't fully understand Paul's
teachings. That's a pretty powerful warning, especially

when one consider these were the very last words Peter penned!

What's the big mystery Paul taught? That God Himself now lives in us! This unique revelation is meant to set us free in our hearts, minds, emotions, habits and lifestyle. Paul continually emphasized what Christ did for us and what Christ is doing in us. We are not merely forgiven sinners like Old Testament believers were. The New Testament believer is born again! The Early Church understood these Pauline truths that defeated the devil and brought lost souls rushing into the Kingdom of God: "Christ lives in me" (Colossians 1:27) and "I am anointed" (2 Corinthians 1:21) with the same Holy Spirit Jesus was! Today it would almost seem egotistical to agree with these Scriptures Paul wrote. After 2,000 years, these New Testament truths have been lost to much of the Church.

Paul or Jesus?

There is no small debate in the theological world whether or not Paul invented Christianity as we know it. However, Paul was not the first person to introduce the teaching that God came to live in man. No! Jesus was (John 10:30-34, 14:16-23)! Jesus said He was the "Christ," the "Anointed One," which in plain simple English means, "God lives in me!"

The religious crowd wanted to crucify Jesus, not for being a good teacher or doing good works, but for having the audacity to claim, "God lives in me" (John 10:33). How little we hear this bold confession today. When we say we are "Christian," we are actually saying "God lives in us" and "God has anointed us, too!"

The label "Christian" literally means "Little Christ." It

was a new word coined by non-believers after they saw the followers of Jesus in Antioch, a city of ancient Syria (present day eastern Turkey). These believers reminded them so much of their Master, the Lord Jesus Christ, that they decided to call them "Little Christ's" or "Christians" (Acts 11:26).

To be a Christian means far more than changing religions, joining a church or being forgiven of sins. It means Christ has transformed us to be so much like Himself that we can legitimately be called His Body and we can truly represent Him on this earth. Paul was commissioned to explain this message to the Body of Christ.

> But when it pleased God, who separated me from my mother's womb and called me through His grace [why did God call Paul?], to REVEAL HIS SON IN ME, that I might preach Him among the Gentiles, I did not immediately confer with flesh and blood [in other words, 'I didn't seek man's approval to speak this revelation in public.'] — Galatians 1:15-16

Paul further said:

> I have been crucified with Christ; it is no longer I who live, but CHRIST LIVES IN ME... — Galatians 2:20

How little we hear this kind of talk today, "Jesus is in me! That's why I have the power and ability to help you."

We need to major on this great revelation that God and man are in total union in the Person of Jesus Christ AND in every person who comes to experience the New Birth. When we become Christian – when we are born again – God comes to live in us through the Person of the Holy Spirit! That means we have His Life, His Nature and His Ability inside of us. That is why the Apostle John could confidently declare:

> Greater is HE WHO IS IN ME, than he who is in the world. — 1 John 4:4

The day we fully realize that God lives in us, we will no longer worry or live in fear, but our prayers will become full of boldness and power. This is not merely a "Pauline revelation." This is the "New Testament revelation." This is what Christianity is about! Christ demonstrating His Life, His Nature, and His Power to the world through Christians.

3

WHY DID YOU COME, JESUS?

Day 3

*S*o many Christians believe Jesus came only to forgive our sins. Yes, forgiveness is a part of the great redemptive work of Christ, but it is not all of it. Why did Jesus come? Let's see what the Master had to say.

> **The thief [satan] does not come except to steal, and to kill, and to destroy. I have come that they may have LIFE, and that they may have it more abundantly. — John 10:10**

What did Jesus mean, He came "that they may have life"? Jesus was talking to people who were physically alive, so He could not have meant that He came to make them physically alive. The word translated "life" is the Greek word "*Zoe*". Zoe refers to spiritual life or eternal life. This is the God-kind-of-

Life. It is the same kind of life God enjoys in Heaven – a life that is above sin, sickness and satan.

No, Christians are not immune from being tempted with sin, attacked with sickness, or persecuted by satan's messengers, but we can have victory over every temptation, sickness or persecution that comes our way. That should not surprise us because Jesus taught us in the Lord's Prayer to pray, "Your kingdom come. Your will be done, on *earth* as it is in *heaven*" (Matthew 6:10, emphasis added).

There is no sin, sickness or satan in Heaven, therefore our bodies, our homes, and our churches can be free of sin, sickness and satan because we have Zoe Life right now, and Zoe is the very Life and Nature of God. It is the very substance that is in God.

> In Him was LIFE [Zoe], and the LIFE was the light of men. — John 1:4

> For as the Father has LIFE [Zoe] in himself; so has He granted the Son to have LIFE in Himself. — John 5:26

> We know that we have passed from death to LIFE because we love the brethren. He who does not love his brother abides in death. — 1 John 3:14

The reason no religion, tradition or superstition can guarantee us eternal life is because they do not have it. Only God has Zoe Life. Only God can impart it to us.

Jesus Christ alone promises to come to live inside the believer and thereby transform our hearts with His Life and Love nature. We are not *going* to pass from spiritual death to spiritual life. We *have passed* from spiritual death to spiritual life the moment we have Christ living on the inside.

One reason we know we have Zoe Life right now is we sense that divine Love came to live inside of us. Once we receive this Life, it becomes impossible for our born again spirits to ever hate anyone again. This Life is strong. This Love is unselfish.

It no longer matters what the "old you" used to be like and how the "old you" used to respond to circumstances. The old self is dead and the new you is alive in Christ. You can forgive. You can love. You can face that person or situation with Christ's nature in you. You can gain such an awareness of this Life that problems which used to make you give up seem to not bother you any more. You can laugh at adverse circumstances and declare, "I have the Life and Nature of God in me! Nothing can overcome this Resurrection Life and this Love Nature of Christ in me!"

When this eternal life entered into me, there were immediate spiritual and even physical changes. My eyes looked brighter, and this is noticeable in "before and after" photos of me. My pimples cleared up. My lungs began to feel clean. I did not stop smoking immediately after becoming Christian. As I meditated on the Scriptures I am about to show you in Chapters 5 through 9, it was not long before I quit smoking (about 3 months).

Just as importantly, I found myself unable to swear like I used to, and suddenly able to apologize and able to forgive everybody, including my own father. I was no longer mad at him. Just like Jesus said of the men who beat him, "They know not what they do," I thought of my father, "He didn't know what he was doing. Had I been in his shoes, young and without God, I might have done worse!" Rather than anger, I felt compassion for him and other relatives. I was mad at the devil for deceiving people in my family. I stopped fighting my own family and prayed Scriptures over them. Most of them became Christian within twelve months!

A major reason for my family's salvation was that I had visibly changed when I received eternal life. Clearly something far more than "joining a church" or "changing religion" had happened to me. The God-kind-of-life was in me. They could see it!

I know an alcoholic who quit alcohol after she was saved and filled with the Holy Spirit. Being saved is receiving eternal life, but being filled with the Holy Spirit is like an overdose of eternal life. The first 120 Christians who were filled with the Holy Spirit were accused of being "drunk" in the morning! (Acts 2:13, 15) This former alcoholic in our church told me, "Quitting wasn't like I was left dry. I didn't feel empty. I had another high to look forward to. I had a higher high."

As a new Christian, she enjoyed praying in the Spirit as it stirred up the Life of God inside her, ushered her into God's Presence, and offered her a replacement. Once she prayed in the Spirit for six hours straight. That may seem drastic, but drastic bondage needs drastic measures. For anyone who wonders can praying in tongues set us free from alcohol, drugs and other addictions, just remember 2 Corinthians 3:16, "...*Where the Spirit of the Lord is, there is liberty.*" Praying in tongues is fellowshipping with the Holy Spirit, that's why physical or emotional freedom often comes with time spent with Him.

Eternal life is not merely a mental concept. It was a spiritual and physical reality in Christ and it should be a spiritual and physical reality in us, too.

I know another dear sister who had an eating disorder, even though she was a Christian since she was twelve. At the age of nineteen she came to Australia, and the change in diet caused her to see herself as "fat and ugly". For nearly three years she ate too little and exercised too much. After she came to our church, she discovered the power of believing and declaring that eternal life was inside of her. She learned that Christ wanted her to use her words to change her situations, just like Christ spoke to diseases and demons and they left. Jesus said to us believers, "*The works that I do [you] will do also; and greater works than these [you] will do...*" (John 14:12). So this sister spoke to her body.

She told her body, "I have fast metabolism and I will weigh this much," and she named the number of kilograms she thought was ideal. As soon as she accepted God's image of her and activated her faith by speaking in line with God's thoughts, she said, "The main thing was fear left me. I didn't fear eating the wrong thing any more. I just ate normally and got to my ideal weight." Knowing you have eternal life is freedom!

> These things I have written to you who believe in the name of the Son of God, that you may KNOW that you HAVE [present tense] eternal life [Zoe], and that you may continue to believe in the name of the Son of God. — 1 John 5:13

Jesus came not only to forgive sins, but to give us His own Life, Nature, and Power. He gave us Zoe Life. We have it now. Say it to yourself: *Eternal life is a present possession for every believer! I have the Life and Nature of God in me now!*

4

HOW TO PUT THIS LIFE TO WORK FOR YOU!

Day 4

*C*hrist has made you a supernatural being full of His life, faith and love, but you need to come and find out what He has done. It is obvious that not every Christian is enjoying the supernatural life Jesus came to give us. The minority of Christians are truly experiencing the full victory. Others seem defeated when they meet sin, sickness or satan. What must Christians do to put this life to work for them?

This eternal life is not going to work automatically for you just because you read this book or hear one sermon about it. You must LAY HOLD of it with your faith and your mouth. Speak some Scripture every day and renew your mind with its truth. Paul told Timothy by inspiration of the Holy Spirit:

> Fight the good fight of faith [how?], LAY HOLD ON ETERNAL LIFE, to which you were also called and have confessed the good confession in the presence of many witnesses. — 1 Timothy 6:12

The problem is that when Christians are born again, their spirits are instantly changed but their minds and bodies are untouched. You understand that when you get saved, if you had brown eyes, they don't become blue, and if your mind never studied Chinese, it isn't going to suddenly become fluent in Chinese.

If you want to walk in the fullness of this eternal life, you will have to do something to your mind and your body. Romans 12:1-2 instructs Christians to "present their bodies as a living sacrifice" and to "renew their minds with the Word of God."

Unless our minds and our bodies yield to that Life and Nature of God inside our spirit, we will not benefit from it in our natural lives. Yes, we can be saved, Spirit-filled, and stuck. It is possible.

We must not only learn how to put this Life to work for us, we must also "unlearn" some unbelief that's become SOP [standard operation procedure] in the Church's preaching and singing. (If you are listening to secular music that stirs up negative emotions in you like anger or feelings of a broken-heart, I would suggest you stop during the next 4 weeks. The Bible talks about different kinds of fasting. I have fasted for 30 days from different things, such as chocolate, TV, news [which is virtually always negative!], and secular music.) There are some Christian songs which I prefer not to listen to or sing. They do not glorify God or agree with the

Bible. Some songs truly damage and rob our faith, such as those that beg for the Holy Spirit to come or ask God for more love or more power. Christians subliminally accept a message of weakness and unbelief by singing and listening to such songs.

The Holy Spirit came on the Day of Pentecost and stayed. He has never left the Church for 2,000 years. The Holy Spirit is here! The power of God is in us. The love of God is poured out in our born again hearts by the Holy Spirit who is given unto us (Romans 5:5). If we are born again and Spirit-filled, we don't need to ask for the Holy Spirit to come or beg for more of God's love and power. We need to use that love and power in the Name of Jesus. We need to yield to that eternal life that is already present in our transformed spirits!

Eternal life is what we have now—it is a present possession. But this revelation is not going to fall on you like rice at a wedding party. You must study it and build it into your consciousness. You have to renew your thinking by looking up Scriptures that tell you who you *are* in Christ, what you *have* in Christ and what you *can do* in Christ.

And you're going to have to speak them, declare them out loud, and as First Timothy 6:12 says, *profess them before many witnesses (KJV)*. Tell people, "I am not the same old person you used to know. That person is dead and gone. I am a new person! I've got the Life and Nature of God in me! Hallelujah!" Tell God, tell yourself, tell the devil, tell the angels, "I can because Jesus lives in me!"

Because my biological father left my mother before I was even born, I rarely spent time with him. The little time he spent with me as a kid, he ended up smacking me hard because I didn't do what he said. That was my memory of him. The little time he spent with me as a teenager, he and I would get into fights and I would call him names. Once I told him, "You have no backbone!" I didn't choose the best time to say that as he was driving at high speed. He literally swerved his car off the highway to give me his fist! I thought we were going to have a car crash and die!

After I got born again in Thailand, I wanted everyone to see that Jesus had changed my life - I no longer cussed, night clubbed, or did drugs. After a couple of years, I had an opportunity to return to Australia, so I initiated a meeting with my father. (We who know God's love have to be the first to reach out to people. Love tries to close the distance. That's what Jesus did for us when we were sinners - He came down to close the distance between God and sinner.) Don't wait for the other side to take the first step! You as a Christian should take the first step!

We went out to dinner with his current wife, and no matter how hard I tried to share God's goodness, he didn't want to acknowledge any of those changes God had miraculously done in me. Instead, he tried to condemn me by reminding me about my past... how terrible I was, how I got so mad, how I lost my temper. The devil will try to use people closest to you to mock you and pull you away from God. "No prophet is accepted in his own country," Jesus said (Luke 4:24 KJV).

Even though I was a new Christian, I had learned enough of the Bible to remember Second Corinthians 5:17. We were sitting across the dinner table from each other, I looked into his eyes with the love of God, and I spoke these words to him, "That Steve you're talking about is dead. Second Corinthians 5:17 says, If I am IN CHRIST, I'm a new creature. Old things are passed away, behold all things are become new!" Till this day I don't know if he understood what I said, but he has never once mentioned my past again.

You see, God's Word has power. We don't need to wait for other people to believe the Bible before we believe the Bible. I quote the Bible to people who say they don't believe it, and the Bible still produces results. God's Word is concentrated truth. People's minds may reject it at first, but people's consciences know it's true. I quoted Second Corinthians 5:17 to my father so he would know:

1. **I agreed with him about my past,** I *was* a terrible sinner (I've learned the best thing to do when people accuse me of something is just to agree with them and move on); and

2. **I am not that person any more.** I died in Christ and have been made alive. I am born again. My past doesn't rule over my future. I am set free!

Once I speak God's Word with love, it's up to God to confirm it. I don't have to worry about my father's words any more. It's so important for us to learn to counter people's unedifying words with God's Word. Faith is nurtured by our declaration of the Word of God.

How will we grow up spiritually?

> But, SPEAKING the truth in love, may GROW UP in all things into Him who is the head - Christ. — Ephesians 4:15

We grow up by speaking the truth in love, not merely by knowing the truth or agreeing with it. We must declare who we are IN CHRIST and what we have BECAUSE OF HIM. We have Zoe Life. We have our Redemption. We have the very same stuff that was in Jesus that made devils cry and sickness leave.

When God wants to revolutionize your life, He starts by changing how you see yourself and how you speak about yourself. He renamed Abram "Abraham" (Hebrew for "father of multitudes") before he had his son Isaac. Abraham had to go around telling his neighbors, "Call me *Father of Many Nations*" when his entire family consisted of him and Sarah living alone. It must have been slightly embarrassing for the neighbors to listen to Abraham, but did God's Word come true? All Israel and nearly all the Middle East trace their lineage to this one father who spoke God's Word: Abraham!

God sent an angel to call Gideon "a mighty man of valor" before he had defeated the Midianite army or done anything valiant in the eyes of his nation (Judges 6:12).

God sent a prophet to call David "king" before he ever set foot in a palace (1 Samuel 16). Locals knew him as nothing more than a shepherd boy.

You might say, "I wish somebody important spoke like that about me!" Somebody very important already has - God! Why not let His words shape how you see yourself and how you speak about yourself? Our personalities are shaped by words. Our destinies are decided through words. God's words decree your destiny more powerfully than anyone else's. You activate the power of His words by believing and speaking them every day.

Here are four more Scriptures that tell us the importance of our words.

66 Death and life are in the power of the tongue: and those who love it will eat its fruit. — Proverbs 18:21

How we should speak differently, more wisely, more gently, when we understand that our words have the power of death and life! I don't think Christian husbands should joke about their wives in a demeaning and embarrassing way in front of other people. A husband has the power to bring life or death to his wife just by the words he speaks.

I don't agree with some parents who joke about how their kids are a "terror" or they look forward to being away from their kids on a holiday. What will those kids think about themselves when they hear they're a burden to their parents? What sort of identity is being formed in such children? Parents have the power of life and death in their tongue.

I like being with my children and I let them know it. My wife and I trained them to be pleasant and helpful. I look forward to more time with them, not less. I want to take them on vacations with me. I know one day they will leave our nest, but as long as they are with us, I express my love, joy and delight over them. They are pleasant kids because we believe and speak that they are helpful, calm and obedient children. No, they are not perfect, but they are being positively shaped by the words we parents speak.

Many parents struggle with their teenagers addicted to the Internet or porn. We will talk about this in detail in Chapter 7. What I have noticed in every case of children hooked on porn is they have low social and communication skills. Their underdevelopment in these areas can be traced to their parents not communicating with them enough or talking over them. The children complain to me that their parents don't listen to them.

You might ask, "What's the connection between low communication and porn?" This may seem simplistic to you, but boys would rather have a real relationship than stare at photos of naked women. Who would want to stare at dirty pictures in a lonely dark room if they could get the real person?

But many children today have not been equipped with life skills. (I offer some mentoring tips and life skills through my blog: www.Cioccolanti.org).

*H*ow should parents communicate with their children specifically about sex and dating?

Here are three common methods which do not count as good communication in our family:

1. **Having the "sex talk".** You know what I mean. The awkward once-in-a-lifetime lecture about no sex before marriage.
2. **Telling them "no dating".** This one gets vociferously repeated as they start to notice the opposite sex or get asked out. The prohibition usually falls on deaf ears because it is just that, a prohibition without much reason or communication.
3. **Asking them, "Where have you been? Why did you come home so late?"** This is not communication and both sides know it. Parents resort to this once the children start dating and the situation seems to be out of your control.

How should parents communicate instead?

1. **You need to make dates with your children to have hundreds of "sex talks" geared towards their age.** Taking them out once a month gives them a lot of life skills. You should constantly affirm their gender. You should keep the doors of communication open and let them know it's safe for them to come to you first. Otherwise they will run to their friends in school or some wrong influence. You can keep an open door by talking at them less and listening to them more.

2. **You should explain to your children why it's not preferable for them to date yet, and when it would be OK to date.** God's reasons are in the Scriptures. Open them and read them together (I provide some in Chapter 7). You may have your own reasons. For me it's a matter of priority and maturity. There is no point for children to date until they have graduated school and can be responsible for another human being. If they are stable and can take care of themselves, then there's no reason why they should not date with the purpose of qualifying someone for marriage. My emphasis in delaying dating is not to spoil their fun or communicate that they're not good enough to date. No! My emphasis is that they are too good to give themselves over to just anyone! Jesus didn't come only to forgive their sins; He also came to give them abundant life in every way! God has made them with a purpose and a destiny, and not every boy or girl who says 'I love you' qualifies to be their life companion.

3. **Once they start dating don't cut off communication!** Many parents go from the one extreme of yelling at their kids about "no dating!" to the other extreme of being completely uninvolved after their kid has a boyfriend or girlfriend. Why not help them plan their dates? Pick out their clothes? Talk about what they're going to do and help them establish good physical boundaries and a reasonable curfew. It would be wise to ask when they go to parties if there was any smoking, drinking, drugs or young couples slipping off into a private room by themselves. You can also verify the story with others who attended the party. Show that you are on their side and that you care.[1]

This is how parents can release the Life of God into their children! Your words are far more important to your children than any of their peers'. God gave you the authority to parent. If you have done it wrong in the past, humble yourself and tell your children you were wrong. Ask for their forgiveness and try to start over. In most cases it's not too late. Children who are well loved and well adjusted socially will seek a good relationship rather than a gross substitute like porn.

> So shall My word be that goes forth from My mouth; It shall not return to Me void, But it shall accomplish what I please, And it shall prosper in the thing for which I sent it.
> — Isaiah 55:11

God's Words are powerful. There is creative power in

God's Word. When God spoke the universe was created. Now when we speak God's Words, we are releasing the most powerful force the world has ever known into our lives and our families. God promises that His words will not return to Him void or empty. In other words, they will not fail. They will produce results.

> This Book of the Law shall not depart from your mouth, but you shall meditate in it day and night, that you may observe to do according to all that is written in it. For then you will make your way prosperous, and then you will have good success. — Joshua 1:8

If we want to enjoy prosperity and success, we must meditate on God's Word, especially the New Testament revelations of who we are IN CHRIST and of the Life of God inside of us! We need to become increasingly aware of what God has truly done for us through the sacrifice of Jesus Christ. He came to give us more than forgiveness of sins. He came to give us eternal life. Major on this revelation and you'll be set free from emotional baggage, addictive bondages, and enjoy a good life. You will live to impart Jesus Christ to others in your world, because Christ lives in you!

> And they overcame him by the blood of the Lamb, and by the word of their testimony; and they did not love their lives to the death. — Revelation 12:11

How did believers overcome obstacles and challenges? By the Blood and by their words. Declare out loud, *"I have overcome all the wicked forces in my life by the Blood of the Lamb and by the words of my testimony.*" Then go tell somebody! Mankind's enemy has been defeated. Death has lost its victory. You don't have to be afraid of death or any other enemy because God overcame them by His Resurrection Life. Then God put that Life into you! Make God's Word a part of your conversation. Give testimony to that victory today!

5

THE 30 DAY MEDITATION PLAN

Days 5 to 11

One of the greatest mysteries about Christianity is summarized in the words CHRIST IN YOU—God is actually living inside you the believer! There are over 100 Scriptures in the New Testament which teach us who we are in Christ and what we have because of Christ. Many of them contain the words "in Christ," "in Him," "in Whom," "with Christ," "through Him," "by Whom," etc. Some of them contain the words "eternal life" or "everlasting life." Others simply tell you of the power God has given you as a believer.

Use these Scriptures! Mark them in your own Bible, personalize them by declaring, "That's mine. God's Word is God speaking *to* me and *about* me!" Speak them on a continual basis over yourself, your family and your church. Faith, like love, needs an outlet of expression. It's not love until you express it. It's not faith until you say it!

A young Christian named Jon Acuff was struggling to admit that his dream was to become an author. Acuff had published some blogs and magazine articles, but he was afraid to call himself a professional. "In the midst of this struggle to find my calling," he wrote, "I had the opportunity to interview Steven Pressfield, author of *The War of Art*. I asked him when a writer becomes a writer, and he said seven words that forever changed the way I thought about writing: 'You are when you say you are.' ...So how do you become a professional writer? Say you are one. Then believe it. And then start doing it."[1]

The next five chapters contain 70 identity-building Scriptures that will show you who you really are, and what God really thinks about you. They work only if you meditate on them. The word 'meditation' in the Bible does not mean to sit in silence or empty your mind. On the contrary, to meditate means to fill your mind with God's thoughts, and then to speak them out.

The Hebrew word for meditation is *hagah* and it means to 'muse' and 'mutter'. To muse is to be absorbed in thought. Musing is related to both music and memory. Biblical meditation includes the elements of 1) thinking, 2) speaking, 3) memorizing, and 4) asking. Many Christian parents train their children to memorize a Scripture a day. Memorizing Scripture should be a part of normal Christian life. Speaking helps you think clearer, memorize faster, and ask better questions. Remember you are when you say you are. The act of speaking is central to meditation.

I recommend that you speak these Scriptures out loud for *at least* the next 24 days. Personally, I have used the Scripture-prayers over and over. I have prayed them for more than 30 days. I have come back to them at different times of my life, whenever I needed a spiritual uplifting or refreshing. So you may wish to repeat these five chapters for a full 30 days or more. I believe that you can break an old habit and form a new one within 30 days. Many people have set a new pattern in their thinking and lifestyle by following this 30-day rule.

As you speak these truths, you will experience freedom and victory in areas of previous hardship and failure. If you will concentrate on these truths, you will be so changed, you won't recognize yourself. If you will build them into your consciousness, then at the first moment of pressure from the devil these Scriptures will rise up out of your spirit and you will speak them out of your mouth. Your mind can be so renewed by these truths you can feel as if you are born again AGAIN! In fact, you are not born again again, but your mind is coming into the reality of what God has done for you in Christ.

The following Scriptures are split into five chapters and are intended to help you get started on declaring who you are in Christ and what you have because of Him. They are listed basically in the order of how they are found in the New Testament. Repeat them everyday for the next few weeks and feel free to look further for other similar Scriptures. You will be empowered and changed by God's Word.

🦋 🦋 🦋

e HIMSELF took our infirmities and bore our sicknesses. — Matthew 8:17

Declare: *He took my infirmities and bore my sicknesses. If He bore them, I do not have to bear them! The devil cannot legally put on me what God laid on His Son—sin, sickness, depression, pain and disease. He bore them for me.*

A disciple is not above his teacher, nor a servant above his master. It is enough for a disciple that he be LIKE HIS

TEACHER, and a servant LIKE HIS MASTER. If they have called the master of the house Beelzebub, how much more will they call those of his household! Therefore do not fear them. For there is nothing covered that will not be revealed, and hidden that will not be known. — Matthew 10:24-26

Jesus said I am not above Him, but I am like Him! I take after my Heavenly Father. I remind people of my Lord (Acts 4:13). The apostle John said, "...as He is, so are we in the world" (1 John 4:17). As far as the devil is concerned, I am just like Jesus, because He is in me. Just as some rejected the Lord, so too some will reject me. I will not allow it to offend or bother me, because I am not above my Master.

Go into all the world and preach the gospel to every creature. He who believes and is baptized will be saved; but he who does not believe will be condemned. And these signs will follow those who believe: In My name they will cast out demons; they will speak with new tongues; they will take up serpents; and if they drink anything deadly, it will by no means hurt them; they will lay hands on the sick, and they will recover. — Mark 16:15-18

Jesus authorized me to be His ambassador. He will open doors for me to tell people why Jesus came. And in the Name of Jesus I am commissioned to cast out devils, speak in tongues, travel without fear of harm, and impart healing to the sick. These signs follow me because I believe in His Name.

Behold, I give you the authority to trample on serpents and scorpions, and over all the power of the enemy, and nothing shall by any means hurt you. — Luke 10:19

The devil is powerless against me in the Name of Jesus. The Lord has given me the "power of trampling" on serpents and scorpions and I trample down all the power of the enemy; nothing shall injure me *(Moffat)*. *No weapon formed against me shall prosper (Isaiah 54:17).*

For God so loved the world that He gave his only begotten Son, that whoever believes in Him should not perish but have everlasting life. — John 3:16

God so loved me that He gave me His only begotten Son, that I who believe in Him should not perish, but have everlasting life. Eternal life is a present possession. I have eternal life now because I believe in His Son now.

Therefore if the Son makes you free, you shall be free indeed. — John 8:36

Jesus has set me free! I am stress-free, worry-free, and care-free. I refuse to let the devil rob me of my freedom. I am free from unforgiveness, false standards of success, fear of public speaking, insecurity, jealousy, depression, pornography, suicidal tendencies. Jesus paid the price for me to live free!

Most assuredly, I say to you, he who believes IN ME, the works that I do he will do also; and greater works than these he will do, because I go to My Father. — John 14:12

Christ has faith in me! Jesus said I would do His works. I can do His works by the same way He did them: through the Person of the Holy Spirit. The same Holy Spirit who anointed Jesus anoints me to do my work. I can heal the sick, raise the dead, and cast out demons. I must be about my Father's business.

I am the vine, you are the branches...If you abide IN ME, and My words abide in you, you will ask what you desire, and it shall be done for you. — John 15:5, 7

All my prayers are answered because I abide in Jesus (when I'm born again) and His Words abide in me (when I do my daily devotional, meditation and prayer). I'm intimately connected to the Lord. Just as sap flows through a plant, His life, faith and love flow through my inner man. His Zoe Life—the Life of God—is in me. His nature—the faith & love nature—is in me.

If the world hates you, you know that it hated me before it hated you. If you were of the world, the world would love its own: but because you are not of the world, but I HAVE CHOSEN YOU out of the world, therefore the world hates you. REMEMBER THE WORD that I said unto you, The servant is not greater than his lord. If they have persecuted me, they will also persecute you; if they have kept my saying, they will keep yours also. — John 15:18-20

My comment: Becoming a Christian means knowing Christ. Since He bore the cross, we will bear a cross. Since He suffered rejection, we will suffer some rejection. Yet He promised His yoke is easy and His burden is light (Matthew 11:30).

I've learned it's very important to discard a spirit of rejection out of my heart very quickly. Dr. Mike Murdock has particularly helped me with some of his wise nuggets, included below. Here is wisdom when you feel rejected:

Rejection is when God hardens the heart of someone He doesn't want in my life. (Think of Pharaoh and Moses.)

Rejection is when God disqualifies someone He knew I wouldn't.

Rejection is divine removal from a place I was too weak to remove myself.

Rejection occurs when God does not want someone in my future.

Rejection cures me of depending on others as crutches and helps me trust fully in God.

Rejection is progress. Thank God for rejection!

The more rejection I experience, the more prepared I will be the moment I find acceptance. The more the rejection, the higher the reward. (Think of the highest position in national government. To be President of the United States, a candidate has to be rejected by roughly 50% of the population who did not want him there and voted for his opponent!) I don't need everyone to like me to succeed in God's eyes.

Rejection is to be expected from those closest to me. Jesus said, "I tell you the truth...no prophet is accepted in his hometown" (Luke 4:24 NIV). My family keeps me humble. My relatives will see my success, but won't let it get to my head. I'll never be a 'big shot' to them. My family is my training. Everyone I need to face in the world is already in my family. God gives me family to prepare me for my assignment.

Rejection is not permanent. "NO" does not mean "never".

Rejection is evidence it's not the right person, right place or right time yet.

Rejection returns my focus on my assignment now.

Rejection saves me time.

Rejection gives me clarity.

Rejection by men propels me to spend more time with God in prayer. Acceptance rarely does. Beware the pitfall of popularity.

❧   ❧   ❧

*T*he glory you gave to me I have given to them, that they may be one just as we are one. I IN THEM and you in me, that they may be completely one, so that the world will know that you sent me, and you have loved them JUST AS you have loved me. — John 17:22-23 (NET) [This was Jesus' prayer to His Father]

God loves me the same way He loves Jesus! There are things I can do to pleasure God, but there's nothing I can do to make God love me less or love me more. He loves me as much as He loves Jesus!

For IN HIM, we live and move, and have our being. — Acts 17:28

Everything alive is in motion. Life moves towards growth and increase. In Christ I am alive, moving, and have my being. In Him I have life, direction and purpose.

Being justified freely by His grace through the redemption that is IN CHRIST Jesus. — Romans 3:24

In Christ, I am freely justified and made right before God.

For if by the one man's offense death reigned through the one, much more those who receive abundance of grace and of the gift of righteousness will reign in life through the ONE, JESUS Christ. — Romans 5:17

I have received abundance of grace and the gift of righteousness. If righteousness is a gift, then I do not have to earn it or deserve it. I receive it as a free gift. I reign as a king in my domain in life through Jesus Christ.

There is therefore now no condemnation to those who are IN CHRIST Jesus, who do not walk according to the flesh, but according to the Spirit. For the law of the Spirit of life IN CHRIST Jesus has made me free from the law of sin and death. — Romans 8:1-2

Because I am in Christ Jesus, RIGHT NOW, present tense, there is no sense of condemnation about me. The law of the Spirit of Zoe Life IN CHRIST Jesus has made me free from the law of sin and death. I walk in love, I walk in the light of that law of Zoe Life, and no germ, sickness, or disease can attach itself to me. I resist the devil and he will flee from me. (James 4:7)

Now if we are children, then we are heirs - heirs of God and co-heirs WITH CHRIST, if indeed we share in his sufferings in order that we may also share in his glory. — Romans 8:17 (NIV)

I've been born in the right Family! I will not entertain the victim mentality or speak any victim vocabulary. I'm an heir with Christ. Many benefits await me as I exercise my rights in Christ and expect God's best. Being an heir carries with it the privilege of sharing both the glory and the suffering of Christ's high status. Even when I suffer, it's because I'm a winner, not a victim.

And we know that all things work together for good to those who love God, to those who are the called according to His purpose. — Romans 8:28

All things are working together for my good, who love God and am called according to His purpose. I will not complain like Job or Jacob, instead I will rejoice that God is setting me up for good, and my latter end will be better than my beginning! (Genesis 42:36, Job 42:10, Haggai 2:9)

Yet in all these things we are more than conquerors THROUGH HIM who loved us.— Romans 8:37

No, devil! You cannot defeat me. I always say "NO!" to the devil and "YES!" to God's Word. In all these things I win an overwhelming victory through Him Who has proved His love for me (Phillips). I face life fearlessly, a conqueror!

[Christ] became for us wisdom from God—and righteousness and sanctification and redemption. — 1 Corinthians 1:30

IN CHRIST I am wise—I have maturity;

I am righteous—I have security;

I am sanctified—I have purity;

I am redeemed—I have identity. I belong in God's Family!

Now thanks be to God who always leads us in triumph IN CHRIST, and through us diffuses the fragrance of His knowledge in every place.

— 2 Corinthians 2:14

Thanks be to God who always causes me to triumph in Christ. I'm grateful to God for leading me to victory. Wherever I go, He makes my life a constant pageant of triumph in Christ, diffusing the perfume of His knowledge everywhere by me (Moffatt).

But their minds were blinded. For until this day the same veil remains unlifted in the reading of the Old

Testament, because the veil is taken away IN CHRIST. — 2 Corinthians 3:14

The veil which blinded the Old Testament saints' minds has been done away with IN CHRIST! His Life enlightens my spirit and increases my mental capacity. (See Psalm 119:97-100.)

Never say again that you are dumb or slow, even if you heard other people say it to you. It is not true! You have been changed by Christ and His eternal life is flowing out of your heart and permeates your mind and body. His wisdom is your wisdom. Believe it and expect it to flow out of you!

6

THE 30 DAY MEDITATION PLAN ~ THE PURPOSE OF FREEDOM

Day 12

66 **Now the Lord is the Spirit; and where the Spirit of the Lord is, there is LIBERTY. — 2 Corinthians 3:17**

*D*eclare: *God gives me liberty, the freedom to choose good or evil, but He wants me to use my liberty to choose Him. The more I follow His leading, the more I desire His Holy Spirit, the freer I will be. True liberty comes from my relationship with the Spirit of the Lord. Jesus said, 'The Spirit of the Lord is upon Me, because He has anointed to Me to...proclaim LIBERTY to the captives...and to set at LIBERTY those who are oppressed.' God wants me to be free!*

Let's meditate on this one Scripture for today. Why is it important for us to be "free"? What are we supposed to do with our freedom? How are we to maintain our freedom?

Since my university days till now, I love reaching out to students on campus. One of the most common objections I hear from students when we invite them to church is, "I don't have time." My question to them is, "Do you have two kids? Are you paying off a mortgage? Working over-time?" No, I'm joking. I don't ask them that because it would be sarcastic. We who are married with children know students have more free time than anybody in the world!

I do ask them, "What would you do if you had more free time? If you feel so restricted now that you cannot afford to put God first, how would you be different if God suddenly gave you more free time? What would you do with this freedom?"

This is not an academic question. Everybody will get a taste of more free time. Everybody will have an opportunity to manage more free time. It may not come the way you like it, but it will come. I've watched adults complain they have no time for God, then when they get laid off work or confined by an illness, suddenly they have lots of free time. What did they do with it?

In just about every case I've seen, they squandered it. The sick Christian did not use their free time to study healing in the Bible or get to know Christ the Healer. The unemployed Christian did not use their free time to enrol in Bible school or attend prayer meetings more regularly. Instead, they could spend six hours a day watching rental movies or surfing the Internet in search for a job. God gave them free time, but they didn't know how to use the freedom.

Most students have some free time. Even with looming assignments and exams, they go out on long dates or for late night partying. Then when they break up with a girlfriend or boyfriend, they are blessed with even more free time.

Instead of using it to improve their lives, some isolate themselves and even blame God for a relationship they shouldn't have begun in the first place. They have not learned how to use their freedom.

*W*hy is it important to be free?

God has a special purpose in our freedom. Seven times God told Moses to command Pharaoh, "Let My people go...!" But that wasn't the end of His statement. God said, "Let My people go, THAT..." The word "that" precedes the purpose of our freedom. God wanted His people free for a reason. Do you know God's reason? He repeated seven times, "Let My people go THAT they may SERVE ME" (Exodus 7:16, 8:1, 8:20, 9:1, 9:13, 10:3, 10:7).

My mentor once asked a sick lady attending a healing meeting, "Why do you want to be healed?" She said, "So I can play tennis." That kind of person is not going to get healed! James said so, "You ask and do not receive, because you ask amiss, that you may spend it on your pleasures." Other translations say, "You ask with wrong motives" (James 4:3). I happen to be a lover of tennis, but God is not going to heal me just so I can go play more tennis! I ought to have better motives than that. There's nothing wrong with desiring to be healed, blessed with a spouse, or set free financially, but we should desire these things so THAT we may serve our Lord MORE.

> Now when Jesus had come into Peter's house, He saw his wife's mother lying sick with a fever. So He touched her hand, and the fever left her. And she arose and SERVED them. — Matthew 8:14-15

Peter's mother-in-law was a wise woman. As soon as she was healed, she did not go play tennis. She knew God heals us so we can be free to serve!

ℰalled to fight for freedom

The subject of freedom is a running theme from the start of the Bible. In the Book of Exodus, we find God wanted to set His people free in order to serve Him. The challenge was NOT getting people to leave Egypt. The challenge was once they were free and walking through the desert, they actually longed to go back to slavery! In a strange way, there is comfort in our bondage. There is familiarity in the former things.

A Christian has no problem with the teaching of freedom. A Christian is willing to be free from addictions and bad habits. Most people long to be free financially. I've seen people spend large sums on investment or real estate seminars (far more than they've ever given to God), wishing to be free from debt or a job they don't like. But when people find out that the path of freedom is not as easy as they originally thought, they tend to go back into debt and previous patterns. When believers find out that the path of freedom includes a walk through the wilderness and a few battles inside the Promise Land, a shocking number turn back to the familiarity of slavery.

Rick Joyner wrote in his book *The Surpassing Greatness of His Power*, "Even though the Israelites were free and moving toward their destiny and fulfillment, when they encountered difficulties, most of them began looking back on the terrible oppression of slavery and wanted to return to it. Herein lies the dividing line that separates those who go on to victory from those who go back to their doom... Those who are free would rather perish in the wilderness trying to fulfill their destinies than go back to slavery. Until we make the decision that we will not go back, we will not go forward."

In order to fulfill the plan of God for our lives, we have to decide we will not go back to our old dating habits, spending habits, or complaining habits. The temptation to go back and date a non-Christian boyfriend or girlfriend can be great. Some parents pressure singles to be married for financial stability or social status, rather than to be in God's will, grow spiritually, and serve God more.

To be in God's will, we have to be set free from the desire to please people more than please God. We have to be set free from wanting human recognition more than God's recognition. There is a false sense of security that slavery offers.

The purpose of difficulties is to cure us from longing to go back to Egypt. A person who has experienced a bad relationship has the fortitude to wait and stay out of relationships that don't improve spiritual growth. Pain is necessary so we know we never want to go back there. Our pain motivates us better than any mentor.

God warns Christians through Israel's example that it's easy to start out right and perish before you get to the promise. Too many believers turn back in their hearts because they think it's easier to get what they want in Egypt.

I've seen Christians leave church for the offer of a job in another city, yet they don't know what church they're going to next or consider if it is God's will. One woman from the Middle East was greatly helped in our church; her children were growing spiritually and her husband had come to faith in our services. But as soon as her husband got a higher paid job offer in another capital city, she encouraged him to take it. I asked if they had prayed about it. They considered the money as a blessing from the Lord and said they could go to church anywhere. I knew they were missing God, but they would not be convinced. They moved to that city where her husband met another woman, committed adultery and her family fell apart. The children's faith in God was never the same, yet it was not God's fault. The parents had missed God. They made money more important than spiritual growth. From God's perspective, his faith was more important than his income.

> But SEEK FIRST the kingdom of God and His righteousness, and all these things shall be ADDED to you. — Matthew 6:33

Putting God first pays. I remember another young girl in our church who was saved out of many addictions. We knew she sometimes turned back to marijuana as a Christian, but we loved her and encouraged her to stick with church even when she felt she wasn't good enough. She had a beautiful voice and started serving on our worship team. She was making new friends and blossoming in her faith. Then she went on holiday to an island in Queensland and came back to tell us she was moving there. She asked me if she should go. I personally like Queensland. They ran a catchy series of TV ads that said, "Queensland, beautiful one day, perfect the next." I could understand why she wanted to up and leave behind her sordid past in Melbourne. It would seem like a fresh start. In the natural, it seemed irresistible.

I asked her had she prayed about what church to go to. She said she was sure there was a good church everywhere and she was going to find one after she got there. I knew in my spirit that is not how God leads His children. God puts first things first. He cares more about our spiritual formation than a pay raise or change of ambiance. I asked her again had she considered if this was God's will for her. But she had already made up her mind that the grass was greener on the other side, or in this case, the state was sunnier on the other side.

Soon after she got to the island she met the wrong people and fell pregnant. The man did not want to marry her or take responsibility for the baby, so she returned to Melbourne a single mum. We know all this because one night God revealed this to my wife in a dream. The young lady did not come back to our church, but others have confirmed the facts. In my opinion, having a baby is never a tragedy, but God's plan for her was far better. There was a fine young man in church, clearly her type, a hunk to many of the single girls, who was secretly in love with her. He wanted to date her had she stayed. But she longed for an island instead of God's perfect will.

It's easy to start walking out of Egypt, but the walk of freedom includes a journey through the wilderness. Getting to the Promise Land is not easy, but it's worth it.

Some singles want to be married so badly that they get discouraged by the wait. They think it's easier to date a spiritually incompatible boyfriend or girlfriend, and hope they will improve after marriage. That's an illusion. If he or she won't go to church with you now or won't pray in the Spirit with you now, the situation will not likely improve but rather get worse after marriage. It's better to wait than to turn back. Don't be discouraged by the wilderness.

When you go through the wilderness, it's because God wants to work something OUT of you. In Israel's case, He wanted to work out their slavery mentality. In your case, it may be codependency, an unhealthy attachment to some-

one, an inculcated shyness, a passive attitude, an unwilling-
ness to open your mouth and communicate.

One young man came to our church with high academic
qualifications, but for a full year he could not get a job or get
a date. Every girl he approached turned him down, and the
best job he landed was an office cleaner working the night
shift. He was walking though his wilderness!

It's hard for some people to understand why God would
allow that to happen when he had just joined church and
started getting serious with God. But God cares more about
who you are than what you have. I often say to people under
my mentorship, "When you're ready, there it is!" If you don't
have it yet, it's because you're not ready for it yet. So prepare
yourself! Get ready!

I told this man to make good use of his free time. Don't
be idle. Don't spend all your time searching for a man to
bless you with a job. Do what you can and serve the Lord as
if He were truly your boss. The Lord is no man's debtor. If
you serve Him, He will reward you!

This man followed my advice, started volunteering
around the church office and ushering faithfully on
weekend services. Shortly after that he landed his dream job
with an airline. (Years later, when thousands of employees
were laid off, he kept his job. Recently he was promoted to
take care of the Prime Minister's plane, the equivalent of
Airforce One in Australia!)

It seemed as if God took His time, but it was sure worth
the wait! He learned to walk in his freedom. With the free
time he had, he chose to put God first, instead of complain
about being unemployed. He used his liberty to make God
Number One.

His next goal was to get married. Even though he had a
respectable job, still he could not get a date. What was the

problem? He finally came to me in his frustration and asked if I saw anything in him that needed to change. Often people will not ask, seek or knock until they have their wilderness experience.

I don't like to tell people what to change unless they ask me. You will find that this is true of most mentors. We don't want to meddle in your business. The moment he came to me and asked, I knew in my spirit what his problems were. I'm not smart enough to know in my head. But God does anoint pastors with supernatural wisdom to help His people.

I told him, "You're a great guy that's got a lot of qualities girls like. You honor your parents, are faithful in church and know how to keep a budget. However, there are 2 things that you need to change." I paused to check if he was still keen to listen. He gave me permission so I continued, "Number 1, you're too strict. You have to lighten up. Number 2, you're too stingy. All the girls you've asked out are turned off by these traits. They are small things to change, and if you do, God will send her."

He didn't take it well. In fact, he was so offended he told me later he thought about leaving church! But having a tender spirit, he went to the Lord and prayed about it. He made the adjustments in these areas and in no time, the woman of his dreams appeared. I married them! Like I said, "When you're ready, there it is!" or "there she is!"

We all have faults and flaws. The wilderness reveals our traits of immaturity which God wants to deal with. He cares about us and has our best interest at heart.

Embrace difficulties as an opportunity to convert your shallow beliefs into rock-solid faith. If you're single, use your freedom as a single to serve God and establish an unshakable pattern of putting God first!

7

THE 30 DAY MEDITATION PLAN ~ SEXUAL FREEDOM

Days 13 to 14

*W*hen you became Christian, you did not merely adopt a new religion or change religions, your sinful spirit was annihilated and a brand new spirit was given to you. You are something the world and your own family have never seen before!

> **Therefore, if anyone is IN CHRIST, he is a new creation; old things have passed away; behold, all things have become new. — 2 Corinthians 5:17**

Declare: *I am a new creation in Christ Jesus. I am a new creation being with the Life of God and the Love nature of God and the supernatural ability of God within me.*

This Scripture is so powerful, I want its power to sink

into you for a moment. We know that there is a number of people who have fallen into the trap of Internet addiction, like over-watching YouTube and looking at pornography. Singles find it a challenge to be free from this addiction as they may feel lonely or constantly have access to the computer. The temptation constantly pops up.

I admire one single man who was set free from pornography after he came to our church and became Christian. I wanted to know how he was set free and asked him about it. He told me, "*2 Corinthians 5:17, when I found out God made me a new creature, I didn't feel like doing the same things the 'old me' used to do any more.*"

It doesn't surprise me that he was set free the same way I was set free - through the power of Scripture. Imagine, just one Scripture is enough to break a lifelong bad habit! What will meditating on all these Scriptures do for you? It will completely transform your personality and renew your identity!

Our areas of temptations may differ, so there is no need to judge one another, but the principle of freedom remains the same. My personal struggle is not with porn. I have seen porn before, as most men have, but personally I think they are disgusting. Yes, I do like to look at beautiful things as any normal red-blooded man would, but porn is not beautiful.

The word "pornography" comes from two Greek roots *porne* meaning prostitutes + *graphia* meaning writings or drawings. Pornography means pictures of prostitutes. Christian men and women would find the idea of soliciting a prostitute repulsive, yet they may not realize that looking at pornography is really a form of prostitution. The person's naked body is no longer private but is open for hire and for use outside of a covenant relationship. Pornography is debasing the dignity of women in particular.

The real purpose of pornography is masturbation. Many Christian ministers have strong views on things which the Bible doesn't say much about, such as masturbation. I cannot find anything in the Bible which talks about masturbation. There is a theological attempt to relate Onan spilling his semen on the ground to masturbation, but this is twisting the Scripture out of context. Onanism is not masturbation. Onanism is withdrawing before ejaculation to deny a woman a child (Genesis 38:9). Since it was Onan's responsibility to take care of his brother's widow, and children were very important to the value of a woman in ancient society, Onan's selfishness was considered evil by God. It had nothing to do with him touching himself.

So what should Christians make of masturbation? Most Christian ministers condemn it. Most secular voices recommend it. I cannot condemn something the Bible doesn't condemn. That is over-reaching my authority and is not the responsibility of a godly preacher or pastor. We represent God exactly as His Word says, at least we must try to.

Nor do I condone masturbation outright. Why not? Because the Bible does condemn lust, and in most cases of pornography, a man or woman is lusting, wasting time, and using their bodies for no good.

What I am against is what the Bible is against. The Bible is against lust. Jesus said, *"Whoever looks at a woman to lust for her has already committed adultery with her in his heart"* and *"If your right eye causes you to sin, pluck it out and cast it from you. It is better to enter into life with one eye, rather than having two eyes, to be cast into hell fire"* (Matthew 5:28-29). The command is mental purity. If you can masturbate without lust, then I am OK with it in moderation. And if you have a wet dream, it's not your fault. Your body can get pent up and tries to find release naturally.

Masturbation is a universal urge that starts very young. Guys talk about it openly, but girls rarely get taught by their mothers, sisters, or anybody in the church. This is a shame. Some girls grow up feeling guilty and condemned about it. I know of girls who discover feelings down there as early as the ages of 7 to 12. Some of them relieve their urges by squeezing their legs together. Boys by the age of 13 will probably have had their first wet dream (unconscious ejaculation in bed). Then they discover strong feelings down there.

Like any urge, you have to bring it under some self-control. Over-eating is destructive. Over-surfing the Internet is destructive. To be sure, over-masturbating is destructive, mainly because the lust will twist your mind and render you incapable of treating a woman in a dignified, non-sexual way.

Sex is a beautiful God-given gift to be enjoyed in marriage. Your sexuality is not wrong. I tell concerned mothers of boys who start liking girls, "Relax. At least you know he doesn't like guys. Better he likes girls, right? You should celebrate it!"

What children need is not our unwarranted criticism, but our support and mentoring. What young people don't understand is that sex is best when there's an emotional connection with the other person. If sex were just a physical act, then you wouldn't need much more than a pillow or your hand. But we know that is a shallow substitute for real sex. What's missing is the emotional bond that takes time to develop.

Trust and the ability to say what we want without fear or shame are powerful aphrodisiacs between two lovers. This type of bonding is what young Christians should learn to develop, through good communication and walking in the God-kind-of-love. When you're born again and married, you are enhanced as a human being and as a sexual being! You are, in truth, far more capable of love than the porn stars.

Freedom in the area of sexuality is central to becoming a healthy human being who is ready for long-term relationships. Too often, singles assume that all their sexual struggles will go away once they're married, but it's usually not true. For some, it may even intensify after marriage. If they don't have self-control now, if they don't deal with their flesh before they meet someone special, this area of weakness will dog their heels all their life.

God would rather you be single and free than hurriedly married and permanently bound. It's better to be a whole person without baggage before you find that special somebody and enter marriage. If you are already married but struggling, there is still hope. Let's take a look at what the Lord taught.

Jesus said you are already clean, but you need to be filled, *"When an unclean spirit goes out of a man, he goes through dry places, seeking rest, and finds none. Then he says, 'I will return to my house from which I came.' And when he comes, he finds it EMPTY, swept, and put in order. Then he goes and takes with him seven other spirits more wicked than himself, and they enter and dwell there; and the last state of that man is worse than the first. So shall it also be with this wicked generation"* (Matthew 12:43-45). Learn these six lessons Jesus taught:

1. **When you are born again, the devil leaves you - the real you - your spirit.** He can never again enter your spirit (called 'possession'), but he may try to come back to tempt your mind (called 'obsession') or attack your body (called 'oppression').

In fact, Jesus warned that the devil will almost certainly try to come back. I say it this way: I served the devil for the first 20 years of my life, and I served him good (I know it's not good grammar, but it's true). I not only sinned, but I also recruited others to sin with me. I'm ashamed to say it now. So when I left the devil and became Christian, it was only natural that he got withdrawal symptoms. He missed me. When he tried to come back to tempt me, I just resisted him until he knew he was unwelcome. I belong to Jesus forever. Nobody likes to go where they feel unwelcome, so don't welcome him with your words!

2. The devil acknowledges that when you become Christian, you are clean, "SWEPT and PUT IN ORDER," according to Luke's account (11:25). You should believe and rejoice God has made you clean!

3. There are unclean spirits whose assignment is to put unclean thoughts into people's minds. The media is overrun with unclean spirits and they don't know it.

"Uncleanness" is a euphemism for homosexuality and sexual perversion in many Scriptures (Romans 1:24, 6:19; 2 Corinthians 12:21; Galatians 5:19, Ephesians 4:19, 5:3; Colossians 3:5), because sexual perversion always starts with an unclean thought that went unchecked.

Homosexuality is *not* genetic; this popular assumption has been discredited through identical twin studies, in which thousands of siblings have the same genes, yet not the same sexual orientation.[1]

Homosexuality starts with believing a lie, that you can't help it and it's OK. Any form of sexual immorality starts with an unchecked thought, unchecked desire, and unchecked flesh. We can stop uncleanness by the power of the Holy Spirit who helps us to control our flesh and say "no!" to unclean thoughts.

Other people have strong urges to eat. It doesn't help them for us to say, "You can't help it. You're born with the urge to eat non-stop." It may be difficult, but everyone can stop. It's for your good and for your health to stop the flesh from ruling over your life.

Homosexuals live on average 25 years less than heterosexuals. I have personal experience with this, having held the hands of homosexuals who died young of sexually transmitted diseases and having had an Australian cousin who was homosexual and killed himself in his 30s. On the basis of mortality, homosexuality is more dangerous than smoking! We live in a free society where it's not any of my business whether you want to smoke or be homosexual, but we should not lie to our children that it's safe and OK. The proper thing to do is to educate children with the truth and let each individual decide based on truthful information. Our media is complicit in this tragedy because it withholds truth and facts that disagree with their secular bias. God doesn't hate homosexuals, He just knows the harm they bring to themselves and others.

4. People can get attacked with unclean thoughts very young. Some estimate that the average age children first get exposed to pornography is now 5 years old. The Bible doesn't skirt this issue of early sexualization of kids. In two instances, a little boy and a little girl in the Bible were oppressed by "unclean spirits" (Mark 7:25, Luke 9:42). In both cases, the families went through agony.

Nothing hurts a family more than sexual violation and sexual perversion. The unclean spirit is the most confusing and deceiving type of demon. It was the only kind of demon that some disciples could not cast out (Mark 9:18). The disciples of today are no different. Most Christians are uninformed about sexuality and most preachers are confused and powerless to deal with homosexuality. Some have even joined the other side and said it's OK, it doesn't harm anyone, they were born that way and can't help it. All lies of unclean spirits.

But we are not powerless. Jesus said, "This kind can come out by nothing but prayer and fasting" (Mark 9:29). You're going to have to fast from pornography and the Internet to be set free sexually. You're going to have to do a little extra praying. Jesus is saying the same thing as He taught in Matthew chapter 12: you're going to have to keep your house clean and filled up with good things. I can tell you that after I pray and get in the Presence of God, I leave with an extra strength, a force field, a resistance to temptation. No, I am not invincible, but the residue of intimate time with God lasts all day. It is strengthening. If you're struggling in the area of sexual sin, make sure to do extra "prayer and fasting." Unclean spirits do not have to rule us. Remember, "He gave them power over unclean spirits, to cast them out..." (Matthew 10:1).

5. When the unclean spirit tries to come back and tempt a Christian, he says, "I will return to MY HOUSE..." Like a scorned lover, he is possessive. Your body was once his house, but now it is the "temple of the Holy Spirit" (1 Corinthians 3:17, 6:19). God does not live in a duplex. He does not share His house with another tenant. You are not an apartment. You are a single-occupancy house, the living temple of a Holy God. Don't let intruders in through the windows of your eyes!

6. Since the believer is clean, how can an unclean spirit come back into his head? The problem was when the believer was set free, he did little or nothing to fill his mind up. When the evil spirit came back, he found the believer "EMPTY, swept and put in order." That's an invitation for demons! No mind can stay a vacuum. Your mind will get filled with something. Better to be clean and filled up with

God's Word everyday - that will keep lust and unclean thoughts away.

When we come to Christ, we are swept and cleaned like a brand new home, but many of us never take the time to fill our new home with good things. Even though God has given us a new home, it can still get trashed out by our old friends or look unseemly because we moved our old furniture in.

Get some new friends! Buy some new furniture! Don't go back to a boyfriend who lusts after you for sex but is too chicken for commitment. Fill your house with good things. Buy yourself lots of Christian books and DVDs. Read, watch, pray. Fill yourself with the Word, never miss church, pray in the Spirit, and the devil will find no place for him to stay.

Sexual purity is possible. Not only will you be happy to be pure and free, so will your spouse and family![2]

8

THE 30 DAY MEDITATION PLAN ~ YOUR TOTAL FREEDOM

Days 15 to 21

🦋 🦋 🦋

*F*reedom Verses for the next 7 Days
The following Scriptures show us that when we become Christian, we are not merely saved from sin, but saved for a noble cause: to serve God and help other people know Him. We are set free for a purpose! We have all been given the same ministry, the ministry of reconciliation, which is expressed in different ways according to our personalities and talents. Freedom is important because no one will fulfill his God-given purpose and destiny until he becomes free.

❝ **All this is from God, who reconciled us to himself THROUGH CHRIST and gave us the ministry of reconciliation: — 2 Corinthians 5:18 (NIV)**

> We are to tell how God was IN CHRIST reconciling the world to Himself, not charging men's transgressions to their account, and that He has entrusted to us the Message of this reconciliation. — 2 Corinthians 5:19 (Weymouth)

Declare: *In Christ, I am reconciled and have been given the ministry of reconciliation. God has made me an agent of reconciliation. As His personal representative, I invite people to "be reconciled to God. God is your friend. God is NOT your enemy." I am ordained to speak the Message of Peace between God and man!*

Now then, we are ambassadors FOR CHRIST, as though God were pleading through us: we implore you on Christ's behalf, be reconciled to God. — 2 Corinthians 5:20

I am an ambassador for Christ. I am an envoy of Christ (Moffatt). I entreat people on Christ's behalf, as if God were exhorting, appealing, and making a request to others by my voice.

For he hath made him to be sin for us, who knew no sin; that we might be MADE the righteousness of God IN HIM. — 2 Corinthians 5:21 (KJV)

I am the righteousness of God in Christ. In Christ, I have status, position and right-standing with God. My standing with God is secure. I can never be more righteous than I am now, because the Righteous One lives in me. In Christ I do not become good; I am MADE good with the goodness of God (Phillips). I can stand before God without any sense of guilt, fear or shame. Therefore I come boldly to the throne room of God (Hebrews 4:16) and obtain what I need. My prayers avail much – my prayers work! (James 5:16).

But it was because of the false brethren secretly brought in, who had sneaked in to spy out our LIBERTY which we have IN CHRIST Jesus, in order to bring us into bondage. But we did not yield in subjection to them for even an hour, so that the truth of the gospel would remain with you. — Galatians 2:4-5 (NAS)

In Christ I have liberty! I will not yield to critical people or participate in their criticism. I refuse to be brought into bondage by false brethren who sow division! I choose to walk in divine love and walk with a clear conscience.

I have been crucified WITH CHRIST; it is no longer I who live, but Christ lives in me; and the life which I now live in the flesh I live by faith in the Son of God, who loved me and gave Himself for me. — Galatians 2:20

I am crucified with Christ. I consider I have died and am now enjoying a second existence! (Knox) The old me is dead and a new me has arisen with Christ. I am dead to popularity and criticism. I am not moved by people's praise or censure. I don't have to try to die. I am crucified with Christ.

Nevertheless I live! Yet not I, but Christ lives in me;. And the life which I now live in the flesh I live by the faith of the Son of God, who loved me and gave Himself for me. Christ is in me!

My comment: I have used Galatians 2:20 many times to bring my flesh under control. I just mutter it to myself quietly and it instantly "kills the flesh". Jesus said "anyone who does not carry his cross and follow Me cannot be My disciple" (Luke 14:27 NIV). I believe quoting Galatians 2:20 is one way to carry the cross and crucify fleshly desires.

For you are all sons of God through faith IN CHRIST Jesus. — Galatians 3:26

Being a child of God requires faith in Christ. I am a child of God through trusting in Jesus.

There is neither Jew nor Greek, there is neither slave nor free, there is neither male nor female; for you are all one IN CHRIST Jesus. — Galatians 3:28

In Christ, we are all one! There is neither Jew nor Gentile, bond nor free, male nor female. There is no racism in Christ. There is no sexism in Christ. There is no looking down on someone else economically in Christ. We are all equally loved and valued in Christ Jesus!

It is for freedom that Christ has set us free. Stand firm, then, and do not let yourselves be burdened again by a yoke of slavery. — Galatians 5:1 (NIV)

The Messiah has set me free so that I may enjoy the benefits of freedom (ISV). Christ has made me gloriously free (Weymouth). I will not be hampered with or held down by a yoke of slavery.

As far as our relationship to Christ Jesus is concerned, it doesn't matter whether we are circumcised or not. But what matters is a faith that expresses itself through love. — Galatians 5:6 (GWT)

In Christ, circumcision is not valid, neither is uncircumcision, but only faith active in love (Moffat), faith acting through love (Goodspeed), faith that finds its expression through love (Knox). Faith works BY LOVE. I choose to forgive and walk in love.

For you have been called to live in freedom, my brothers and sisters. But don't use your freedom to satisfy your sinful nature. Instead, use your freedom to serve one another in love. — Galatians 5:13 (NLT)

God calls me to freedom! I will not use freedom as an excuse to yield to flesh. Rather, I serve others in love.

For IN CHRIST Jesus neither circumcision nor uncircumcision avails anything, but a new creation.— Galatians 6:15

For in Christ Jesus, outward externals are not anything, but a new nature is everything (20th Century New Testament). It doesn't make any difference now whether we have been circumcised or not; what counts is the power of the New Birth (Taylor) – whether we really have been changed into new and different *people (Phillips). In Christ, I have experienced the power of the New Birth. I have been changed into a new and different person. I am a new creation, a man with God living inside me!*

Blessed be the God and Father of our Lord Jesus Christ, who has blessed us with every spiritual blessing in the heavenly places IN CHRIST. — Ephesians 1:3

It is not me waiting on God, but God waiting on me to know and to use all the spiritual blessings, gifts and opportunities He has given to me. I am blessed with all spiritual blessings in heavenly places in Christ. God has made a provision for me – He has blessed me with everything I need. In His mind, they are already mine! In my mind, they are already mine! Glory be to God!

To the praise of the glory of His grace, by which He made us accepted IN THE BELOVED. — Ephesians 1:6

We ought to accept one another, just as Christ has accepted us, welcomed us, and received us (Romans 15:7). Though some may reject me, God accepts me. I have a friendly reception every time I approach God and pray. This access brings glory to Him.

IN HIM we have redemption through His blood, the forgiveness of sins, according to the riches of His grace. — Ephesians 1:7

In Christ I have my redemption. I am not trying to get it! I already have it!

And this is the plan: At the right time he will bring everything together under the authority OF CHRIST - everything in heaven and on earth.— Ephesians 1:10 (NLT)

God is collecting every good thing in heaven and on earth, and bringing them together in Christ. Christ is my Head, so I am part of that gathering together in God!

IN HIM we were also chosen, having been predestined according to the plan of him who works out everything in conformity with the purpose of his will, in order that we,

who were the first to hope in Christ, might be for the praise of his glory. — Ephesians 1:11-12 (NIV)

It's a beautiful thing to be "chosen". God has chosen me to receive His inheritance and His Glory. Because I am in Christ, I have obtained an inheritance according to the counsel of His own will: that I should be to the praise of His glory...I should cause His glory to be praised (NEB)...I should manifest His glory (Knox). By virtue of the New Birth, His glory is inside me!

But God, who is rich in mercy, because of His great love with which He loved us, even when we were dead in trespasses, made us alive together WITH CHRIST (by grace you have been saved), and raised us up together, and made us sit together in the heavenly places IN CHRIST JESUS. — Ephesians 2:4-6

By God's grace I have been saved. When Christ was crucified, I was crucified with Him. When He was made alive – I was made alive with Him. When He was raised up, I was raised up together with Him and made to sit together with Him in Heavenly places. Just as sinners sit with the devil in darkness (Matthew 4:16), TODAY I am seated with Christ at the right hand of God, in the position of highest authority. I am humbly seated with Christ!

For we are His workmanship, created IN CHRIST Jesus for good works, which God prepared beforehand that we should walk in them. — Ephesians 2:10

I am His workmanship, created IN CHRIST Jesus. I am God's own handiwork...recreated in Christ Jesus and born anew (Amplified). What we are, we owe to the Hand of God upon us. We are born afresh in Christ, and born to do those good deeds which God planned for us to do (Phillips). By the grace of God, I am what I am and His grace is not in vain (1 Corinthians 15:10).

And this is God's plan: Both Gentiles and Jews who believe the Good News share equally in the riches inherited by God's children. Both are part of the same body, and both enjoy the promise of blessings because they belong TO CHRIST Jesus.— Ephesians 3:6 (NLT)

I am a fellow heir and of the same Body, and a partaker of the promise in Christ by the gospel. I am an equal partner in God's promise (Phillips).

I can do all things THROUGH CHRIST who strengthens me. — Philippians 4:13

Through Christ, my Lord, I can do all things. He strengthens me. He helps me do what He calls me to do. His ability is my ability! I cannot be conquered. I cannot be defeated. I can do all things through Him.

And my God shall supply all your need according to His riches in glory BY CHRIST JESUS. — Philippians 4:19

Paul said to his ministry partners, all your needs are supplied. I am a tither and a sower, so I believe all my needs are supplied! I take no thought for the cares of the world. I obey the laws of planting and harvesting, and I expect God to open the windows of Heaven for me (Malachi 3:10). I believe God is my Heavenly Father, Christ is my Source, the Holy Spirit is my Treasure! (2 Corinthians 4:7)

He has delivered us from the power of darkness and conveyed us into the kingdom of the Son of His love, IN WHOM we have redemption through His blood, the forgiveness of sins. — Colossians 1:13-14

I am now set free from the authority of darkness, from the power of satan. By virtue of the New Birth, I have and exercise authority over everything that Jesus conquered: satan, sin, sickness, poverty, fear of death, hell and the grave! I have my redemption.

THE 30 DAY MEDITATION PLAN ~ STRENGTH TO OVERCOME

Days 22 to 28

*I*n this last chapter containing Scripture prayers to build your spiritual fortitude, we will start with several powerful quotes from Colossians. The Apostle Paul wrote both Ephesians and Colossians around the same time from the same place (prison in Rome). Many Christians agree that these two books contain the highest revelation of the mystery of the Gospel, which is our union with Christ.

Some say Ephesians emphasizes the Body of Christ, while Colossians emphasizes Christ the Head of the Body. Ephesians emphasizes the believer in Christ, while Colossians emphasizes Christ in the believer. Because union means we are one, Christ and His Body are virtually indistinguishable for practical purposes. Others make this distinction: Ephesians is *didactic* (teaching) while Colossians is *polemic* (attacking). In other words, Ephesians promotes truth while Colossians attacks error.

The mystery which has been hidden from ages and from generations, but now has been revealed to His saints. To them God willed to make known what are the riches of the glory of this mystery among the Gentiles: which is CHRIST IN YOU, the hope of glory. — Colossians 1:26-27

This is the highest mystery to the Gentile nations – CHRIST IN ME – the hope of glory! Christ is revealing Himself to the world through me.

We proclaim him, admonishing and teaching everyone with all wisdom, so that we may present everyone perfect in Christ. — Colossians 1:28 (NIV)

In Christ Jesus, I may be presented perfect – not merely "mature" – but perfect because the perfected Christ lives in me! When I got born again, my spirit became perfect in God's sight and the perfected Christ came to live in me!

To this end I labor, struggling with all his energy, which so powerfully works in me. — Colossians 1:29 (NIV)

I can labor, striving according to His working, which works in me mightily. If Christ-in-Paul worked mightily in Paul, then Christ-in-me works mightily in me.

My goal is that their hearts, having been knit together in love, may be encouraged, and that they may have all the riches that assurance brings in their understanding of the knowledge of the mystery of God, namely, Christ, — Colossians 2:2 (NET)

I am knit together in love with my brothers and sisters in Christ. I am encouraged and assured of my union with Christ. I understand the mystery of God.

IN WHOM [Christ] are hidden all the treasures of wisdom and knowledge. I say this so that no one will

deceive you through arguments that sound reasonable. — Colossians 2:3-4 (NET)

I am rich because of Christ in me. I will not let anyone entice me with doctrines of devils which sound reasonable, but rob my faith or put down our place in Christ. Jesus paid too high a price for me to feel low about myself or live a religious, defeated life.

Be careful not to allow anyone to captivate you through an empty, deceitful philosophy that is according to human traditions and the elemental spirits of the world, and not according to Christ. For IN HIM all the fullness of deity lives in bodily form. — Colossians 2:8-9 (NET)

I will not allow anyone to captivate me with human philosophy and tradition, no matter how many degrees they have or how many letters appear after their name. I follow Christ, Creator God in human flesh. If Jesus were not fully God and fully man, then God and man could never be united. But because Jesus is fully God and fully man, God can also live in me! O, hallelujah!

Therefore do not let anyone judge you with respect to food or drink, or in the matter of a feast, new moon, or Sabbath days - these are only the shadow of the things to come, but the reality is Christ! — Colossians 2:16-17 (NET)

This Scripture settles it! I will not let my relationship with Christ be based on or affected by what I eat or which day I worship. Some may think these externals are the reality, but real spirituality is in Christ. I am holy, spiritual and close to God because of Christ, not because of what I eat or don't eat, or which day I go to church! Christ is real to me every day of the week and every meal of the day. I'm free from false standards of religion. My faith is not in food, but in Christ.

For the Lord Himself will descend from heaven with a shout, with the voice of an archangel, and with the trumpet of God. And the dead IN CHRIST will rise first.

Then we who are alive and remain shall be caught up together with them in the clouds to meet the Lord in the air. And thus we shall always be WITH THE LORD. — 1 Thessalonians 4:16-17

In Christ, I shall rise with a new resurrection body! I'm going to have a rejuvenating make-over and I'm going to like it.

Rejoice always, pray without ceasing, in everything give thanks; for this is the will of God IN CHRIST Jesus for you. — 1 Thessalonians 5:16-18

In Christ, I rejoice always, I pray without ceasing, I make it a habit to thank God for everything (Williams). I refuse to take my blessings for granted. I am a thankful person. For this is the will of God – this is what God expects of me in Christ Jesus (Phillips).

The grace of our Lord was poured out on me abundantly, along with the faith and love that are IN CHRIST Jesus. — 1 Timothy 1:14 (NIV)

In Christ, the grace, favor and lovingkindness of our Lord abounded beyond measure, overflowed and flooded my life, together with faith and love. Faith and love are in Christ, therefore faith and love came into me in full tide the moment Christ came into me.

For God has not given us a spirit of fear, but of power and of love and of a sound mind. — 2 Timothy 1:7

God has not given me a spirit of fear. I'm not timid, intimidated or easily frightened. I refuse to be called 'shy'. Shy is not godly. There's not an ounce of shyness in Jesus. Jesus was bold. I have the same Spirit as Christ - the Spirit of power, love and a sound mind!

My comment: Fear is an enemy that must be conquered through love. 1 John 4:18 says, "...perfect love casts out fear..." Dr. Mike Murdock wrote in *The Holy Spirit Handbook*, "Fear stops you from *reaching*...Fear stops you from *asking*...Fear stops you from *admitting*...The Holy Spirit is an enemy to fear." Jesus faced much opposition and injustice, yet He refused to fear.

Declare: *I reject fear! Fear cannot remain in me because God has not given me the spirit of fear and the Holy Spirit has given me the fruit of love which casts out fear. Because God loves me, I fear nothing.*

He saved us and called us with a holy calling, not according to our own accomplishments, but according to his own purpose and the grace that was given to us IN THE MESSIAH Jesus before time began. — 2 Timothy 1:9 (ISV)

In Christ, I have been saved and called with a holy calling, not according to my works, but according to His own purpose and grace, which was given to me IN CHRIST before time began.

Hold on to the pattern of wholesome teaching you learned from me - a pattern shaped by the faith and love that you have IN CHRIST Jesus. — 2 Timothy 1:13 (NLT)

I live by faith and love which are mine IN CHRIST Jesus (NEB).

You therefore, my son, be strong in the grace that is IN CHRIST Jesus. — 2 Timothy 2:1

I am strong in the grace that is IN CHRIST Jesus.

Yes, and all who desire to live godly IN CHRIST Jesus will suffer persecution. — 2 Timothy 3:12

Rejection helps me understand what God goes through. Jesus said, "All men will hate you because of me, but he who stands firm to the end will be saved" (Matthew 10:22). Paul said the godly will suffer persecution from the ungodly. When some people reject me, I'm in good company!

Who Himself bore our sins in His own body on the tree, that we, having died to sins, might live for right-eousness—BY WHOSE stripes you were healed. — 1 Peter 2:24

God laid on Jesus not only our iniquities and sins, but also our sicknesses and diseases. By His stripes I was healed! God's Word tells me I was healed 2,000 years ago by His stripes. If I WAS healed, then I AM healed. Healing belongs to me because I am in Christ.

You are of God, little children, and have overcome them, because He who is in you is greater than he who is in the world. — 1 John 4:4

I am of God. I am born of God. I am in the Family of God. I am in union with Christ. Because I am in Christ, the Greater One lives in me. He is Greater than the devil. Greater than disease. Greater than circumstances. And He lives in me! Because He lives in me, I am an overcomer. I can overcome satan no matter where I meet him or what the test.

By this we know that we abide IN HIM and He in us, because He has given us of His Spirit. — 1 John 4:13 (NAS)

The Holy Spirit gives me unshakable confidence that I belong to the Family of God! The Holy Spirit confirms in my heart that Christ dwells in me. The Holy Spirit bears witness with my spirit that I am a child of the Most High God. (Romans 8:14-16)

And this is the testimony: that God has given us eternal life, and this life is IN HIS SON. — 1 John 5:11

God has put eternal life into His Son, then He put His Son into me. I have eternal life now! It is a present possession that makes me a supernatural being on earth.

As you share the faith you have in common with others, I pray that you may come to have a complete knowledge of every blessing we have in Christ. — Philemon 1:6 (GWT)

Every good thing is in me because I am in Christ Jesus (KJV). There is a wealth of good things in me that comes from Christ Jesus! (Taylor)

But also for this very reason, giving all diligence, add

to your faith virtue, to virtue knowledge, to knowledge self-control, to self-control perseverance, to perseverance godliness, to godliness brotherly kindness, and to brotherly kindness love. For if these things are yours and abound, you will be neither barren nor unfruitful IN THE KNOWLEDGE OF our Lord Jesus CHRIST. For he who lacks these things is shortsighted, even to blindness, and has forgotten that he was cleansed from his old sins. Therefore, brethren, be even more diligent to make your call and election sure, for if you do these things you will never stumble; — 2 Peter 1:5-10

In Christ, I am not barren or unfruitful, idle or unproductive. I am actively advancing towards a full knowledge of Christ. So I add to my faith:

virtue (power, energy—faith must have demonstration),
knowledge (intelligence—faith must be used intelligently),
temperance (self-control, restraint, discipline—faith will control my tongue),
patience (commitment, endurance—faith is patient),
Godliness (character, God-like attributes—faith is obedient, choosing the will of God),
brotherly kindness (preferring others above self, godliness in action—faith is considerate of others), and
charity (divine love—faith works by love).

Each of these builds on each other:
It takes faith to demonstrate God's power.
It takes experience with God's power to become knowledgable or spiritually intelligent.
It takes intelligence to exercise self-control.
It takes self-control to be patient.

It takes patience to be godly.
It takes godliness inside to show brotherly kindness outside.
It takes acts of kindness to forgive others and walk in love at all times.

This growth is possible by faith in the fact that Christ lives in me with all His faith, power and attributes.

If these things are in me and abound—if I do these things—I will never stumble or fall away (NLT). Never, ever! Instead, I will be fruitful and sure of my calling! I will not forget what Christ has done for me. Because of my growing knowledge of 'Christ in me,' I will never be defeated in life. I am growing in Christ.

❧ ❧ ❧

Therefore lay aside all filthiness and overflow of wickedness, and receive with meekness the implanted word, which is able to save your souls. But be doers of the word, and not hearers only, deceiving yourselves. — James 1:21-22

I am a doer of the Word. God's Word must be received humbly, with meekness, to change my life. I humbly apply every sermon I hear and every lesson I learn. Instead of speaking like the world, I will keep speaking God's Word.

Beloved, I wish above all things that thou mayest prosper and be in health, even as thy soul prospereth. — 3 John 1:2 (KJV)

Father, You wish ABOVE ALL THINGS that I prosper. My soul is prospering by the Word and by prayer, therefore I also prosper financially and walk in health. The blessing of the Lord makes me rich, and He adds no sorrow with it (Proverbs 10:22). The more I love people, the more important prosperity becomes to me. I long to do more for my loved ones, for my church, for orphans, widows and missionaries (James 1:27, Matthew 25:36, I Timothy 5:17). Bless me indeed and enlarge my territory! Let your hand be with me, and keep me from harm so that I will be free from pain. And God granted my request (I Chronicles 4:10 NIV, Prayer of Jabez).

And [He] has made us kings and priests to His God and Father, to Him be glory and dominion forever and ever. — Revelation 1:6

Jesus is the King of kings and the Priest of priests. I am one of those kings and one of those priests. I am royalty being groomed for rulership and ministry. Because of Jesus, I am a ruler of my domain in life and I stand in the gap for the lost in my nation. Glory and dominion be to Him forever and ever. Amen.

10

IT'S GOOD TO BE FREE!

Day 29

*H*ow to Stay Free
Scripture-prayers played a big part in my personal freedom as a Christian. Continuing the habit of praying Scriptures helped me maintain my freedom. *O, it's good to be free!* Just as I have kept these 70 Scriptures within my reach till this day, so too you can keep this booklet with you for as long as you need it. You can keep referring to the Scriptures in the previous chapters during your hour of prayer or daily devotion to God. I have read these Scriptures on my feet and on my knees, in my home and outside my house, publicly and privately. Even on vacation I have taken these Scriptural affirmations with me. Truth never gets old.

From time to time, you may not sense the feeling of victory. You may even feel as if God were far away. That is a normal experience as a believer. Don't think you have dwindled in faith, you may in fact be growing in your faith! Jesus said, "Thomas, because you have seen Me, you have believed. Blessed are those who have not seen and yet have believed" (John 20:29). In other words, some people believe God only because of their feelings, but others believe God in spite of their lack of feelings. Which is the higher form of faith? Clearly Jesus commended the one who doesn't need warm fuzzy feelings to trust God! "For we walk by faith, not by sight [or physical senses]" (2 Corinthians 5:7).

When I feel the need for more strength emotionally or physically, I turn back to these Scriptures that built me up in the first place. Pretty soon I will sense the peace of God again... not because it ever left me, but because my mind became filled with other things. Feelings do not determine faith. I can believe the truth regardless of how I feel. But when my emotions become a cluttered room in my soul, it becomes hard for me to hear God's assurance clearly. When life gets out of balance, when I need to find my center of gravity again, I revisit these Scriptures to remind myself what God thinks about me.

After fifteen years of pastoring church members, I am aware how desperately people need freedom from their past, whether childhood hurts or a recent relationship breakdown or some harsh words spoken over them. I do not want to over-simplify spiritual growth and emotional freedom. Speaking Scriptures is one important step to freedom, but it's not the only step.

Grow Deep and Grow Strong

Every step of obedience is a step towards freedom. Because God loves us so much, everything He tells us is meant to help us. A simple act of obedience like water baptism or communion can bring great blessing. Anything God tells us to do, just do it! Obedience to God always carries a reward. It pays to obey.

You will not be confessing these 70 Scriptures forever, though you should revisit them from time to time. Building your spiritual identity through speaking selective Scriptures will always be vital to freedom from inner conflict and oppressing thoughts. But declaring these Scriptures is not the only thing that will make you strong.

Speaking the "in Christ" Scriptures is like targeted healing, but there should also be a general discipline to maintain spiritual health. Just as natural growth will not happen unless you eat and exercise, so too spiritual growth will not happen without a routine. You should have a daily devotion with God, with the goal of reading the entire Bible once every year (eating) and writing down how you will be different that day (exercising). This is one way to grow deep and grow strong.

Spiritual growth, like natural growth, happens in *quantum leaps*. The greatest growth spurts for a human occurs between the ages of 0-1, then 8-13 for girls and 10-15 for boys. In the same way spiritual growth tends to come in spurts.

For me, I have had three major growth spurts. Though your experience will be different from mine, I offer you what I went through as lessons you may learn from and apply in your own way.

❧ ❧ ❧

First Quantum Leap
My first growth spurt occurred when I not only read someone else's book about "who I am in Christ,"

but I made a decision to search, write down, think about and speak out loud the Scriptures that relate to "who I am because of what Christ has done for me." That was the first thing that helped me grow by leaps and bounds.

You may find other Scriptures that speak to your situation. Highlight them. Type them down if you have a computer. Organize them in categories according to what you need. Before our children were born, my wife and I found, typed up, and printed on a sheet of paper a set of Scriptures promising us godly, healthy children. We spoke them before our children were ever born. It's amazing to see how those words have come to pass!

When my mother needed to buy a house, we searched Scriptures in which God promised land and houses. God promised that people who obey Him will lack nothing (Deuteronomy 6:11, 8:9, Psalm 23:1, 34:10). We had an entire sheet of Scriptures. We declared God's Words over the house and even though my mother lost the bid for the house during the auction, the real estate agent came back to her to make one last offer. She got it for the price she wanted and was able to pay cash.

We can be inspired by other people's stories, but the real change takes place when we change. Hearing other believers' stories ought to drive you to search the Scriptures for yourself. God wants us to hunger for Him.

🦋 🦋 🦋

Second Quantum Leap

My second growth spurt came when the Lord told me to go to Bible School and I obeyed. I am not recommending that you immediately go to the nearest Bible School in your town. I know some people who went to

Bible School and they came out worse. That was not my case.

Some Christians I have met should not have gone to Bible School, either because God did not call them to or because they should have gone but they attended the wrong one. My criterion for choosing a school is very simple. I don't judge a school by how many PhD professors are teaching there. By that standard, Jesus would have failed to start or teach at a Bible School! I believe studying under Jesus and the Apostles would have been the very best education, don't you? Yet none of them had a PhD, so that cannot be the most important criterion.

My first criterion is how many graduates go on to do something useful for God, especially winning souls, starting churches, and going on missions. My former Bible School has graduates in 190 countries who are starting churches somewhere in the world every single week. The teachers themselves have won souls, started churches and lived on the mission field. I don't want theorists to teach me because they are like Pharisees. They say but don't do. Worse than that, I have noticed that people who do nothing are most likely to criticize people who are doing something! Their job becomes critique. Their students become critics. What an unfortunate waste of time.

That is one side; let me bring a balance by showing you the other side. My experience with Bible School was very positive. I studied under humble and anointed Bible teachers for 3 hours a day, 5 days a week. I volunteered in a clinic for sick people to meet Jesus as Healer for 1 hour 4 days a week. I attended Bible study on most Wednesday nights and church service every Sunday morning. Besides my own reading, studying and watching Christian videos, I easily spent 840 hours a year directly under the teaching of

God's Word (counting 40 weeks in a school year). My Biblical training lasted 2 years, so all up I spent a minimum of 1680 hours under the Word of God. That resulted in my second growth spurt.

Compare that to the average Christian attending church once a week. If church service lasts 2 hours, and 1 hour of that time is dedicated to the teaching of God's Word, then the average Christian is getting about 52 hours of Bible teaching a year. How much time would it take them to receive the same amount of spiritual input I received in 2 years? They would need over 32 years!

That means I received in 2 years what the average Christian ordinarily take 32 years to learn! And the tragic fact is many Christian don't even attend church once a week any more, so they are getting even less. Then they expect to conquer demons and overcome problems with so little spiritual input – it is a bit unrealistic!

Spiritual growth and personal freedom must be maintained with a consistent habit of attending a home church, plus I would recommend your having at least one other point of contact during the week, be it a cell group, prayer meeting, worship practice, evangelistic outreach, etc. Hebrews 10:25 (GWT) tells us, "We should not stop gathering together with other believers, as some of you are doing. Instead, we must continue to encourage each other even more as we see the day of the Lord coming."

If you are looking for a church that's perfect, I'm sorry but you will find none. Even if there were one, it would cease to be perfect the moment you walk through the doors, because you would bring your imperfection with you!

We must be on guard against the deceptive spirit of perfectionism. Parents who try to raise kids with perfectionist demands end up damaging their personality and ability to relate to God and people. They grow up with a performance attitude. They are convinced that God or people will accept them only if they do good. But rather than doing good, perfectionists tend to procrastinate, get over-whelmed with the big picture and find it hard to finish their tasks, because inside there is a deep-seated fear of failing and being rejected. This kind of strict attitude not only damages children, but also relationships in church. We are to be excellent people, but not perfectionist.

It is precisely in the imperfect environment of a family that we learn our most valuable lessons in life, such as love, forgiveness, communication, reconciliation, and teamwork. It is also in God's Family that we become whole and mature as a people. Without being part of a local church family, you will find it impossible to go through one of the stages of growth spurt God has planned for your good.

While I attended Bible school, I never once skipped church. I don't say this to condemn you if you have ever missed church for a valid reason. I chose to be in church every week because God commanded me to set aside one day out of seven to honor Him. Even though I was enrolled in Bible School, I did not feel like I was learning enough from my classes to get by without church. I felt like I didn't know enough and I had to be a sponge for more of God!

My encouragement to you is: go to a good Bible school if you can, but if not, go to church at least once every week, and twice is better. Don't skimp or skip out. We all need personal ministry and spiritual input regularly in our lives. No matter who else we may be learning from, such as the Internet or TV preacher, we mustn't neglect learning from our own pastor who knows us personally. No, you may not be best buddies with your pastor or get to hang out with him every week, but when the time comes for you or your family member to get baptized, or prayed for, or married or buried, the TV preacher isn't going to come help you, is he? You need the benefits of having a local pastor. He or she is God's gift for your growth and protection.

If you've been hurt by a previous leader or pastor, you need to forgive the leader and let the offense go. He or she may have repented before God, so we have no rights to hold grudges against anybody God has forgiven. People change, so don't hold a bitter image of somebody that will sabotage your own freedom! Tell God your feelings and move on. You may have to swallow your pride, but it's better to obey God and keep a tender heart!

If you're a leader and you have been hurt by people in church, the same goes for you. People may not think about it, but every leader is outnumbered by followers, so I am convinced there are a lot more followers hurting leaders than leaders hurting followers.

God's followers hurt Him even though He never hurt them. All leaders will experience some rejection and betrayal in the course of trying to lead. But as I said, people change. One former church member, a pastor's son, left my church and sent me a critical email. I could have responded to him with a Biblical correction of all his points. But I just prayed for him and wished him the best. About six months later he took a course on forgiveness and freedom and apologized to me. He said, "I want to officially say sorry to you. I should have never left church that way. I should have said encouraging words to you. From now on, I will say encouraging words to you."

I said to him, "I didn't think much about it. But since you said it, I officially forgive you." You see, people grow and change. Give them a chance! Hasn't God given us a chance we didn't deserve?

. . .

*H*ow to Find the Time

Before we go to my third growth spurt, someone may be objecting, "Is it realistic for me to get 1680 hours of Bible teaching to become strong spiritually? Hey, that may work for you, you're a Bible teacher, but I just don't have the time!" I understand your predicament. Let me respond with two comments.

Firstly, like you, I had to intentionally find time to study the Bible. I did not do it solely to become a teacher, but primarily to understand more of the Bible. Knowing God more is beneficial no matter what our call or career. Consider it an investment in your future!

God has given some of you time to study the Bible and you did not know it. Whenever you are in transition, in between jobs, or unable to find work, it may well be the ideal time for you to enroll in a Bible study course in your church, or to find a suitable Bible school for you.

Secondly, my standard is apparently lower than the New Testament's. How much time did the twelve disciples spend in training with Jesus? They spent all day and night with Him. Assuming they slept twelve hours a day (they probably slept less!) and spent only twelve hours a day with Jesus, then the disciples spent 4,380 hours a year under the mentorship program of Jesus. Their training lasted three and a half years, totaling 15,330 hours with the Lord Himself. How long would it take the average Christian who attends church only once a week to learn what the twelve disciples learned? Over 294 years! That's how Jesus prepared twelve world changers. We have a bit of catching up to do![1]

11

UNSHAKABLE FAITH

Day 30

*R*eview
  We grow gradually by eating God's Word and exercising our faith in it. But we will undergo stronger growth spurts by taking certain actions. My first growth spurt came when I decided to look up Scriptures that build my identity, personalize them for myself, and speak them for more than 30 days. This new habit transformed the way I see myself and I am convinced it allowed God to use me more than I could have imagined!

Had I been complacent about my words, had I not taken the Scriptures seriously, I would still have been a Christian, but a stagnant one at best. Too many believers feel stuck in a rut and stressed out like unbelievers. It doesn't have to be so. By finishing this 30 day program, with the help of the Holy

Spirit, you have shared a similar experience which transformed my personal world!

My second growth spurt came when I attended Bible School for 2 years. Learning from humble instructors transformed my life. Spiritual training is essential to fulfilling our destiny. I spent 1680 hours under the direct teaching of God's Word, which is equivalent to 32 years of Sunday church services! The 12 disciples spent about 15,330 hours with the Lord, which approximates 294 years of attending church once a week! Unfortunately some Christians expect to become champions by attending church once a week. People expect so much for putting in so little.

In this day and age, I would say that the best opportunity for your spiritual training will be church-based. You don't have to go far, but you will have to meet with your church family more than once a week to catch up!

Third Quantum Leap

My third growth spurt has come through serving people. There is a saying: "We only learn what we teach others." Serving is learning. Helping others has helped me grow tremendously. Ministry is a part of God's plan for our growth and success.

Speaking Scriptures was essential to my transformation. So was Bible School. But nothing could have prepared me to grow up like the trials I faced while serving people. I have experienced personal betrayal, a church split, and family hardship like I never imagined I would have to experience as a Christian. Thank God we don't have to suffer sickness because that is a work of the devil (see Acts 10:38, Luke 13:16, John 10:10), but we do have to face trials and tribulations because we live in a fallen world. Pain motivates us faster than any mentor. God will use suffering to mould our character. Please ponder these seven Scriptures.

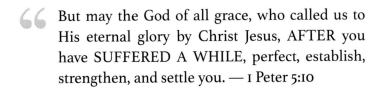

> But may the God of all grace, who called us to His eternal glory by Christ Jesus, AFTER you have SUFFERED A WHILE, perfect, establish, strengthen, and settle you. — 1 Peter 5:10

What is it that will perfect, establish, strengthen and settle us? *Suffering a little while!* No suffering is joyful while you go through it, but know that for Christians no suffering lasts forever. And for Christians, no suffering is senseless. God allows us to go through some things not to destroy us, but to establish, strengthen and settle us.

Trials in themselves will not produce faith, but trials will test whether our faith in Christ is genuine. I am a better minister because of the suffering I have gone through. I react less to criticisms. When I hear a problem, I withhold judgment and try to understand both sides first. I am less moved and less emotional today about things that may have rocked my world, caused me to panic, or made me feel devastated years earlier. I believe that is part of true emotional freedom. The devil is more afraid of me because I have been battle-hardened. This is a part of God's plan for every Christian to be free from fear and free from the devil.

In the Old Testament, Jewish believers were regularly taught that they had enemies to overcome. I believe this is a teaching that has been tragically lost among certain segments in the Body of Christ. Christians seem surprised by criticism and opposition. Some cannot even take it for God's glory, but instead give up.

The Jews were constantly reminded that they were surrounded by enemies. After Moses died, Joshua led Israel into the Promise Land. But Joshua too died before all their enemies could be conquered. The writer of the book of Judges put it this way.

> Now these are the nations which the Lord left, that He might test Israel by them, that is, all who had not known any of the wars in Canaan (this was only so that the generations of the children of Israel might be taught to know war, at least those who had not formerly known it). — Judges 3:1-2

God had an enemy in Heaven - Satan. Since God is training us to rule like Him, we also have to face enemies in life. It's a certainty! God is training us to reign with Christ in eternity. As part of that training, we need to learn to conquer pride, overcome the rebellious spirit, and win over temptations. Pressures and trials in life are necessary to prove that we are worthy of ruling over whatever God will put us in charge of, but we know it includes ruling over angels (1 Corinthians 6:3).

Whatever lies on the other side of Eternity, we will need to be people who can take orders and not be easily offended by others. That makes sense because there will not be a second Fall or a second Redemption plan, so everyone who enters the Kingdom must avoid repeating Satan's rebellion and Adam's disobedience. Satan never saw what an enemy of God looked like because he was the *first* enemy of God. We have an advantage over Satan because we see daily what enemies of God look like, and it's not pretty. We have to defend our freedom from such enemies!

We will also need to be people who will love everyone like God does and not easily fall into pride. That's also understandable since people in this life can fall into pride over the smallest things like increased income or popularity in the eyes of a few human beings. What would happen to such people if they were to be elevated by God Himself or inherit true wealth beyond earthly imagination? To prevent us from falling into jealousy over other people's blessings, God allows some people to be jealous of us in this life, so we will never be jealous of anyone in Heaven. Christians are definitely not merely waiting to die and go to play harps on clouds; we are being groomed for eternal prizes that will be far beyond anything we have ever experienced on earth!

Paul gave us this glimpse into our future.

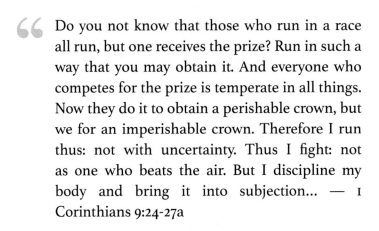

> Do you not know that those who run in a race all run, but one receives the prize? Run in such a way that you may obtain it. And everyone who competes for the prize is temperate in all things. Now they do it to obtain a perishable crown, but we for an imperishable crown. Therefore I run thus: not with uncertainty. Thus I fight: not as one who beats the air. But I discipline my body and bring it into subjection... — 1 Corinthians 9:24-27a

Paul knew that to get the eternal prize, he had to learn to be tough. He had to take criticism and move on. He had to not be so thin-skinned. Despite the rejections he received from his own people, and ultimately the death sentence from Emperor Nero who beheaded him, his influence has outlasted all of the Roman Emperors' combined and his name is forever etched in Heaven's Hall of Fame.

We must face enemies in life. It is good for us. This is what Paul tried to pass on to all Christians. When he and

Barnabas were on a missionary journey and revisited the Christians they had previously taught, they went about:

> Strengthening the souls of the disciples, exhorting them to continue in the faith, and saying, 'We MUST through MANY TRIBULATIONS enter the kingdom of God.' — Acts 14:22

They did not say we *might* have to go through a *few* tribulations. They said we *must* go through *many* tribulations. Our reward is a refined spirit that's qualified to rule with Christ over everything God made!

> Not only so, but we also rejoice in our sufferings, because we know that SUFFERING produces perseverance; perseverance, character; and character, hope. And hope does not disappoint us, because God has poured out his love into our hearts by the Holy Spirit, whom he has given us. —Romans 5:3-5

Suffering for our faith in Christ is nothing to be ashamed of; instead it's something we are called to rejoice in! Suffering is God's way of developing our endurance and character. When we suffer like Christ, we will become strong like Christ. This is ultimate freedom from Satan and all his bondages. Satan had absolutely no hold over Christ. Satan also has absolutely no control over us whose characters are Christlike.

> Though He was a Son, yet He learned obedience by the things which He suffered. — Hebrews 5:8

If Jesus the perfect Son of God had to learn obedience through suffering, how much more we should learn obedience by the things which we suffer.

> And having been perfected, He became the author of eternal salvation to all who obey Him. — Hebrews 5:9

If Jesus could not be perfected in His humanity without suffering, then we too will not be totally free without suffering injustice and overcoming it with love. When we forgive, like Christ forgives, we are set free from our enemies.

The greatest enemy against us is fear. Fear of failure. Fear of rejection. Fear of being alone. When you face a fear and conquer it, that fear dies and the power of Satan is lost in our lives. I notice that in my years of ministry, I cannot stay complacent long. God will always give me a new challenge that stretches my faith a little bit more. I remember the first time I faced a crowd of 10,000 people, the stage seemed so high, the lights so bright, the fear that came upon me was overwhelming. I could have quit. I wanted to just walk out and ask somebody else to speak.

But I thought to myself, "God hasn't brought me this far to quit." I pushed through that barrier of fear and now I can stand comfortably in front of thousands. A room of one or two thousand seems small to me. But not until I suffered and experienced a breakthrough. God will continue to stretch my faith, like being on TV and whatever else that comes. For sure, He wants us to be constantly growing in faith and dependence upon Him.

Remember, God has not brought you this far for you to quit here. You may have to push through to have a breakthrough. Like a marathon runner who wants to quit when she hits "the wall"[1], you have to *expect* the wall and *trust* God for grace to push on through. When your faith seems shaken, and you decide to push on through, your faith becomes unshakable! You have faced the enemy and tasted sweet victory. You have suffered and are no longer afraid. You begin to live in true freedom . My friend, your race is not from the starting point to the wall; your race is from the start, through the wall, to the finishing line. That's where you and I get the prize!

NOTES

4. How to Put This Life to Work for You!

1. These tips and more in Chris Spradlin's free ebook *Sex Lust & XXX*, *www.EpicParent.tv*.

5. The 30 Day Meditation Plan

1. Acuff, Jon, *The secret to becoming a professional writer*, posted 15 June 2012. http://www.jonacuff.com/blog/the-secret-to-becoming-a-professional-writer/

7. The 30 Day Meditation Plan ~ Sexual Freedom

1. Tay, John Dr., *Born Gay? Examining the Scientific Evidence for Homosexuality*, 2010, p48-57, citing numerous studies in both America and Australia, including *Bailey & Pillard (1991), Bailey et al (1993), Kendler et al (2000), Bailey et al (2000)*, all of which confirm homosexuals are not "born that way" or "have no choice". Genetic determinism has been debunked, everybody has a choice, yet the public is largely misinformed by about these findings. Science and the Bible agree: we have a choice!
2. Watch Steve Cioccolanti's one-hour DVD on *"Sexual Identity: Myths and Facts"* available at www.discover.org.au/bookshop

10. It's Good to Be Free!

1. Steve Cioccolanti lectures in Bible schools. Watch some of his DVDs which offer the same content delivered in a good Bible School. Four recommended curricula:
   Bible Introduction: How Did We Get the Bible? (3 hours)
   4000 Years of History: From Creation to Christ (12 hours)
   Book of Revelation (10 hours)
   End Times (6 hours)
   Available from Discover Media, www.discover.org.au/bookshop.

11. Unshakable Faith

1. "The Wall" is a common experience for marathon runners who feel like giving up at a certain distance. It is usually the 20 mile mark when glycogen stored in the muscles and liver are depleted, and the body has to tap into stored fats to convert to energy. When runners push through this barrier, they get a "second wind" and reach the finish line!

VIDEOS BY STEVE CIOCCOLANTI

7000 Years of Prophecy (1 hour)
End Time Complete Pack (58 hours)
6000 Years of History & Prophecy (3 hours)
4000 Years of History (Old Testament Survey,
12 hours from Creation to Christ. Our #1 Bestseller)
22 Future Events Predicted by Revelation (4 hours)
Jewish vs Christian Dating & Parenting (2 hours)
Where is God During Tragedies? (2 hours)
4 Steps to Enter into Your Call (1 hour)
Why Am I Not There Yet? (1 hour)
Atheists Don't Exists (3 hours)
The Life of Joseph (6 hours)
Defeating Fear (3 hours)
Book of Job (2 hours)
Jezebel (2 hours)

Browse DVDs and CDs at: www.Discover.org.au
Watch videos-on-demand at: vimeo.com/
stevecioccolanti/vod_pages

OTHER BOOKS BY STEVE CIOCCOLANTI

From Buddha to Jesus
(Available in English, Cambodian, Chinese, French,
Indonesian & Thai)
ブッダからイエスへ
(From Buddha to Jesus | Japanese Edition)
30 Days to a New You
(Compact Plan for Personal Growth & Freedom)
12 Keys to a Good Relationship with God
(Children's Book written with 6-year-old daughter Alexis)
A Guide to Making a Will
(& Considering a church in your legacy)
**The Divine Code: A Prophetic Encyclopedia of Numbers,
Vol. 1 & 2 (Combined Volume Special Edition)**
(Discover the meaning of numbers)

All e-books are available through Amazon.com.
The Divine Code available as a 2-in-1 set only at
Discover.org.au

★ ★ ★ ★ ★

**Trump's Unfinished Business:
10 Prophecies to Save America**
(Make America Godly Again!)

Paperback
or
Ebook

★ ★ ★ ★ ★

FROM BUDDHA TO JESUS

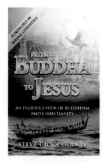

English

Chinese

French

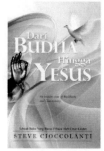

Indonesian

Thai

Cambodian

Available in 6 langauages!

ORDER ONLINE! www.discover.org.au

30 Days to a New You
Now available in Spanish!

MEET STEVE CIOCCOLANTI

Steve Cioccolanti, B.A., M.Ed., is a four-time #1 Best-selling author on Amazon. With over 48 million views, he is one of the most watched Christian YouTubers worldwide.

Watch and subscribe here:
www.YouTube.com/DiscoverMinistries

Born in Thailand to a family of Buddhists, Catholics, Methodists, and Muslims, Cioccolanti has a unique perspective and practical insights into spiritual life. He leads an international church and ministry in Melbourne, Australia.

Having travelled to more than 45 nations, Cioccolanti is a sought after speaker on hot topics such as end-time prophecy, Biblical justice, world religions and breaking news. He is currently authoring more books, filming more videos, and sharing Biblical truths around the world.

Get Mentoring Online!
www.DiscoverChurch.online

Share your story with Discover Ministries at
www.Discover.org.au/testimonies

To partner with Discover Ministries:
www.Discover.org.au/Give

To book Cioccolanti for your church or event contact:
info@discover.org.au

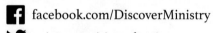 facebook.com/DiscoverMinistry
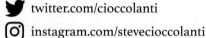 twitter.com/cioccolanti
instagram.com/stevecioccolanti

Made in United States
North Haven, CT
30 November 2022